Creating your life on your terms is really about allowing for grace through your next transition.

LIFE ON YOUR TERMS

The Support You Need to
Follow Your Passion from
Inspirational Entrepreneurs

by Shann Vander Leek

True Balance Press

Published by True Balance Press, a division of True Balance Life Coaching, LLC; Suttons Bay, Michigan

For information on discounts for bulk purchases, please contact True Balance Press at books@ truebalancepress.com.

Library of Congress Control Number: 2010931522

ISBN-13 978-0-9844559-0-4

ISBN-10 0-9844559-0-6

Cover and Text Design by: Mike Kazmierski, Kaz Creative

Chief Editor: Amy McIntosh

Editor: Bryna Rene, Aphrodite, Inc.

Editor: Kelly Kazmierski

Transcription by: Amy McIntosh

Promotional Design: Mandy Palmer, Gruve Design Studio

Contains the author's story of transition, as well as interviews with 41 inspirational entrepreneurs who have created their lives on their terms, found liberation, and are living their dreams.

1. Entrepreneur 2. Transition 3. Passion 4. Trust. 5. Self-Realization 6. Life on Your Terms 7. Dream 8. Inspiration 9. Courage 10. Support

Manufactured in the United States of America.

10 9 8 7 6 5 4 3 2 1

DEDICATION

It requires profound vision to see the path of liberation. To these entrepreneurs who seek to lead us to personal freedom, this book is respectfully dedicated.

IN GRATITUDE

To my generous family and friends.

To Thomas, for your infinite support, patience and loving kindness.

To Marin, for your shiny creative wonder.

To Mom and Dad, for treating me like a superhero.

To Amy, for stepping up and sharing in the enormity of this project.

To Tonya, for being the best data pixie on the planet.

To Mike, for art direction and graphic design wizardry.

To Mandy, for happily creating extraordinary promotional designs.

To Amy, Bryna and Kelly, for editing the hell out of this,
and making this divine creation flow.

To Diane, Deb and Charlie, for coaching me through
the most significant transition in my life thus far.

To Matt, for believing in me, and for stepping up to film
the *Life on Your Terms* documentary.

FOREWORD

When Shann first contacted me and asked if I would be willing to do an interview for her book, I thought, "Sure, no problem. This should take just a few minutes." Then, we spent over an hour on the phone. It seemed like every couple of months I'd get an e-mail about updating the interview, doing a follow-up interview, reviewing the write-up of the interview...

This few-minute project seemed like it was getting very in-depth, and receiving an incredible amount of attention and focus. And thank goodness for all of us that Shann was driven to create something of genuine value.

Thanks to her efforts, she has crafted a book that is an absolute gem.

If you are in the process of creating a life on your terms, the stories in here will inspire you greatly. And that's important. One of the pieces of advice I always share with people who have read my books, and who ask me about moving their life in a more positive direction, is to feed themselves a healthy dose of inspiration every day.

We become what we surround ourselves with. The stories, energy, and messages we allow into our lives have a profound impact on our state of being – which means if we want to live inspired lives, it's very helpful to feed ourselves inspirational sources.

Lucky for us, Shann has provided a giant buffet of inspiration through the content in this book. I suggest reading through the entire book once, then going back to it at least once a week to enjoy another serving. It will feed your desire to live life on your terms, and your belief that it can and will happen.

If you are already living life on your terms, the content in here will bring back happy memories of your own adventures, and inspire you to push for new heights.

Life on Your Terms is waiting for you. So get reading, and with the inspiration you'll find, get living!

- John P. Strelecky

#1 Best-Selling Author of *The Why Cafe, Life Safari,*
The Big Five for Life – Leadership's Greatest,
and *How to be Rich and Happy.*
Find John at www.bigfiveforlife.com

CONTENTS

LIFE ON YOUR TERMS

I woke up in a dreadful fury. The red light on the alarm clock glared at me: 5:30 a.m. A few more minutes of sleep was all I wanted – anything to put off going back to the office.

Does this sound like your average day? It used to be mine.

For many years, I had enjoyed my job, but now it felt more like a prison sentence, and I knew I had to find a way to escape. I decided that I deserved to follow my creative calling. It was time to get real, face my fears, develop a critical path to transition and become the master of my own destiny.

That's how this whole thing started.

My personal career transition sparked my curiosity. Every day, I observed people bumping around from one role to the next, one task to the next, seemingly dead inside. It made me ask myself: how have so many people become cut off from a Universe filled with abundance and wonder?

The delightfully curious creature in my head started to tease and taunt me with questions:

- What if I could talk to wildly successful entrepreneurs who have figured out how to fully leverage a life of entrepreneurial freedom, happiness, tranquility and passion?

- What if together these entrepreneurs and I could identify common threads amongst these visionaries who have summoned the courage to push through the keyhole and gain access to the shiny world on the other side?

- What would happen if I distilled these entrepreneurial characteristics into an inspirational guide?

- If I was able to create a life filled with abundance and passion, and if my personal story was inspirational to others, then wouldn't a collection of stories be even more powerful?

- What if I shared my story, and the stories of entrepreneurs who are living life on their terms, with just one person, who might tell one friend? Would the wisdom begin to spread across the global landscape?

It was these questions which guided me to write this book, which I hope will inspire even just one person to find the courage to follow his or her heart, and to live fully, with complete abandon.

The more than forty interviewees selected for this project are strong entrepreneurial spirits who are highly successful and passionate about their lives and careers — an eclectic cross-section of coaches, artists, authors, CEO's, creatives, directors, videographers, marketers, brand creators, bloggers, life assistants, and intuitives. They come from places around the globe, including Oregon, Michigan, New York, New Jersey, Rhode Island, Ohio, Vermont, Florida, California, Hawaii, Idaho, Asia, The United Kingdom, Canada, and Australia. All are extraordinary people who, through epiphanies or multiple nudges, managed to uncover, identify, and clearly see where they belong in this great big world.

A quarter of the way through the interview process, I knew I was onto something much greater than I'd imagined. Not only are the people involved gracious, kind and bright: they are torch-carriers for the rest of us.

Each inspirational, life-changing story made its indelible impression on my heart. Through the entire process, I felt I was in the presence of greatness. The enthusiasm exuded by each creative, courageous individual was an honor to experience. Truly, these men and women are unfiltered creatures of the universe, following their natural rhythms through freedom's pass. And here, in this book, each of them opens up to share their own personal brand of brilliance.

From chucking it all and backpacking around the world, to not being afraid to die; from never tasting a meal in the same way again, to conquering cycles of mental illness; from climbing the corporate ladder, to base-jumping off the top into the realm of personal freedom: these are the tales of individuals desiring to be their best, giving back to their communities, allowing for divine love – even traveling to remote areas of the world to uncover stories of elephant whisperers. Each stands today, transformed by their own transitions, passions and legacies, reaching out with arms wide open, saying, "Come join me, and the best is yet to be!"

Imagine a life orchestrated to complement your natural rhythms; a life where your work is your play, and your play is your life. You deserve to be happy, healthy and wealthy. You have permission to create your life on your terms. So instead of putting up with mediocrity, waiting for a knock on the door or an invitation to change, take your life's adventure to heart. The process begins here, now, today.

If you are looking for rags-to-riches stories, this book is not for you. More often, it's about giving up material riches to gain natural richness and wonder, or finding the courage to embark on an individual journey while overcoming obstacles with grace. It's about finding a genuine passion for life and accepting the nature of things as they are.

The book is divided into chapters leading through the stages of lifestyle and career transition, with individual interviews supporting the commentary. These true stories of entrepreneurial greatness are intended to spark your curiosity and inspire you to explore your own liberation.

This journey began with my personal transition and reinvention. It is my hope that it will lead to yours. You want to live your life on your own terms. You want to follow your passion without being chained to someone else's dream. You are ready to move forward in the direction of your choosing.

I wrote this book for you, potential entrepreneurs: it's time to get moving – to wake up, lift the veil of the status quo, and embrace the richness of a full life!

CHAPTER I

The Writing is on the Wall

*"Any transition serious enough to alter your definition of self
will require not just small adjustments in your way of living
and thinking but a full-on metamorphosis."*

- Martha Beck

Not too long ago I made one of the most important decisions of my life: to leave corporate America and give my entrepreneurial calling a shot. Somewhere along the way, the corporate culture I was immersed in had changed to a game of ego-driven micro-management, and I began to experience a slow and certain suffocation.

I went through many phases of self-examination, doubt, fear, and suffering before I finally realized it was time for a significant change. Today, I understand that without the extreme discomfort my former work environment caused, I might have never allowed myself to embrace my passion and follow my dreams – but at the time, it was, to put it simply, hell.

The first phase – realizing that change is on the horizon – can be very uncomfortable. A significant shift is coming: you can feel it. You can taste it. Yet you still may not quite be able to wrap your head around it. The more you try to fight transition, reason with it, or think about it logically, the longer you'll stay in that place of discomfort.

There are several telltale signs that it's time to move on. Maybe you wake up one day to find that you're just going through the motions; that you are no longer challenged or even interested. Maybe you wake up every day in a state of anxious dread, or plagued by illness. Maybe you're unnerved by corporate decisions, or you're no longer willing to jump through flaming circus hoops for a paycheck. These symptoms all indicate that the job is killing your soul, and it's time to find a way out.

What does going through the motions look like? Sometimes it's hard to recognize when you're just "bumping around" while you're still bumping around. You may feel confused, fearful, angry and scattered. You may distrust your own decisions, and feel more worried or anxious than normal. The pain of an uninspired work life lends itself to a reactionary autopilot protection program that only makes things worse. We are meant to create, enrich, and enjoy our lives. Living on perpetual autopilot does not serve anybody well.

If you are no longer interested in or challenged by your current position, why stick around? Several of the entrepreneurs I interviewed for this book felt that they hung on to positions longer than they wished because their jobs gave them a sense of security and ease. Why leave a perfectly good job with great pay and benefits just to chase a dream? Trying to be logical and practical, they were blown off course.

The messages with which our parents, teachers and mentors conditioned us drive us to stay committed and loyal. Combine this sort of mental programming with insecurity and self-doubt, and the pain can be almost unbearable. Often, people who really crave change still choose to stick things out a little longer, hoping for a miracle. Some settle for counting the days until retirement.

If you're starting to rack up more sick time than usual, it's a good sign that you're losing interest in your career, or getting worn down by the Powers That Be. As a manager and leader of a sales force for eleven years, I've seen plenty of evidence to indicate that loads of sick time usually means the end of employment. Toward the end of my corporate life, I, too, found myself looking for reasons to be missing in action. This complete reversal of my prior "company first" attitude only added fuel to my smoldering entrepreneurial fire.

Another common indicator that it's time to make a change is, well, *change.* Do you feel like a fish out of water in what used to be a very comfortable environment? For me, a regime change took me from a state of near autonomy to one of micro-scrutiny. In other words, I went from being the golden child to a cover girl with a giant pimple. And yet, I stayed, because fourteen years was a long time to hang with a company, and as much as I detested the new management, I loved my sales force, my six-figure income, and my role as an inspirational leader.

I convinced myself that my presence mattered because I was there to motivate my staff and shield them from upper management's madness. (On a side note, it was a compliment for me to learn that, after my departure, my choice to leave made waves within the organization. Several people, including my direct supervisor, left within months after I took my own first steps on the path to liberation!)

A large part of the eight-to-five workforce seems to have accustomed themselves to a certain amount of suffering. The suffering in Big Corporate America is even worse. It's as if people are trying to buy security with the currency of their own pain. But let's ask all the people who have been laid off in the last several years about "security." Old-school conditioning tells us to get a good job, climb the corporate ladder, save for retirement, and enjoy ourselves in our golden years. Maybe that method worked, once, but it doesn't hold any water in the twenty-first century. You cannot live for the promise of a day in the future.

When we discover that security is an illusion, happiness becomes all that matters. How many times do we need to witness others' regret, or carry shame about missed opportunities, before we're ready to make a change? Do we want to lead lives where we stifle our passions instead of following them? And what about being present for our families? How many parents with children grown and gone remind us to enjoy the journey now?

All we have is this moment. We get to decide whether we want to spend our time making a life, or dancing in a cage for a paycheck.

One big red flag for change is that you've been putting your life on hold. Are you waiting for your tenth anniversary watch/clock/golf clubs before moving on? Are you putting off having children, or taking a life-changing adventure vacation, because you "can't afford" to be away from your desk? If so, ask yourself what you're really waiting for. Maybe the world outside the cage is bigger and scarier than you remember, or maybe it's that golden handcuff that's weighing you down.

John P. Strelecky, #1 Best-Selling author (and participant in this project) created a program called "The Big Five for Life." The idea behind the program is that we should all take the time to create a life plan, including five things we must do before we leave this Earth. It's a very cool concept. So ask yourself, right here, right now: what are your Big Five? Have you taken steps toward achieving any of them, or do they feel more like pipe dreams than real goals? What would your life look like if you could design your ideal situation?

Another sure sign of impending change is the feeling that you must make a difference in the world. The paycheck and the benefits are no longer enough. For me, a major turning point was the realization that selling television commercials does absolutely nothing meaningful for the world. Advertisers spend gobs of money to promote products like Viagra and Lipitor, so that the general public can keep an erection and eat cheeseburgers. Wow! I discovered that I was no longer willing to be part of an organization which had no interest in a healthy corporate culture, which was teeming with politics, which had no interest in human kindness but loads of interest in perpetuating pain and suffering. What had once felt like home to me was now just a big pile of nasty.

This wasn't an easy truth to swallow: I had invested much of my life in the advertising business, and I loved the game – until I didn't anymore.

Hey, people change.

In fact, we are all changing every day: evolving, growing, and learning; researching, soul searching, and witnessing our lives. But these are small changes, accomplished over time. If you want to make a big change, begin by focusing on your current scenario. Where are you right now, in relation to where you want to be? What do you need to get from point A to point B? For example, you might find you need further education, experience, or certification. You may need to save a specific amount of money to cover your expenses before taking a big leap. You may just need time to wrap your head around the idea of leaving the only career you've ever known – and that's fine. But when your life is more miserable than happy because you no longer fit into the confines of your career, it's time to a) get a new job, or b) become an entrepreneur.

Your exit strategy begins with getting your financial affairs in order. If you are the primary earner, you will need a solid twelve-month plan, as well as a firm date to cut the cord. When I decided I wanted out, I was the primary income producer in our family. My husband had to be completely on board for me to make a leap. More than this, he needed to be willing to step up and embrace a lot more financial responsibility. I am grateful for his never-ending support and encouragement: without that steadiness at home, success would have been much more difficult.

Next, you'll want to determine your education and certification needs. If your current job offers tuition reimbursement, can you take advantage of this before your established leave date? Or, can you work out some other way to get the knowledge you need to take the next step, without sacrificing your financial plans?

Your freedom strategy will be a little different than anyone else's, because your idea of freedom is different from anyone else's. But no matter what route you decide to take, remember that you are not alone. Many before you have walked this path. Their stories, and their spirits, are amazing. Enjoy the first group of interviews with inspirational entrepreneurs who have blazed a trail for you.

John P. Strelecky

"Fight for your limitations and they become yours."
- Richard Bach

At the age of thirty-two, John P. Strelecky left a very successful career behind and set off to backpack around the globe. It proved to be a smart choice. His experiences on the road taught him about life, about himself, and about his place in the world. When he returned almost a year later, he was a different person.

Shortly after his return, he had another life-changing experience – one which he credits to the new state of being into which his travels had transported him. He sat down at a computer and his hands began to move on their own, in stream-of-conscious typing. Over the next twenty-one days, each time he sat down, the words flowed through him from somewhere else, and out onto the computer screen.

Although he was involved in the process, John wasn't dictating the process. Not once during those twenty-one days did he read what he had typed. Nor did he think about what to type before sitting down. He simply sat, and allowed the words to flow through him.

The end result of this process was an inspirational story called *The Why Cafe*. It has since been published in nineteen languages, and has become a number one best-seller.

John's experience was particularly unusual in that he had never written anything of length before, and had no formal training or ambitions as an author.

What inspired you to become an entrepreneur?

From a very early age I was aware that I wanted to make it on my own. I come from a moderate-income family and I have two

LIFE ON YOUR TERMS

sisters, and I knew that sending us all to college would be a big burden on my parents. So I started working when I was twelve, with the intention that I wanted to make my own way. Traditional employers won't hire twelve-year-olds, so my only option was to be an entrepreneur.

I started by doing things like painting houses and other physical work. Then, I owned a lawn service. Basically, I'd do the things most adults didn't want to do. Since I was twelve, I charged a lot less than other people, and since I was very determined, I tended to do a better job than them, too.

Once I hit sixteen, I took on regular jobs also, but I quickly realized that the problem with a regular job was that my income was determined by how much time I put in, not by how good of a job I did. As long as people did okay they wouldn't get fired, and if I did an incredible job, I still got paid about the same as the okay person. I saw that the only way to get paid more in a regular job was to put in more hours, and that was problematic, since as a student, my free time was sort of limited.

I guess my entry into the world of entrepreneurship was built on two things. The first was necessity, because of my situation. The second was that it seemed like the best way to achieve what I needed to achieve.

How have you created your life on your terms?

That's a story that requires a little bit of history.

After working hard to save enough money, I entered college when I was about eighteen. I wanted to see the world, so I decided to go to an aviation-focused school and become a pilot. Aviation training is very expensive, so even though I had saved up enough money to start the program, I ended up going to school during the day and working at night.

Between my junior and senior years of college, I received what I thought was my big break. I was selected to participate in a non-paid internship program for a top airline. It was a huge decision for me, because summers provided me with a chance to work and save enough money for the upcoming school year. To work for free for an entire summer meant I'd have to take out some large loans in order to stay in school. At the same time, the internship was a huge opportunity to move forward with my career as a pilot.

I decided to do the internship, and by the time the summer was over, I was one of only two people in the history of the program to receive the top recommendation.

Fast-forward a few years. After graduating and flying for some low budget flight operators, I went back to formally interview as a pilot with the airline I had interned with. One part of the interview was a full medical exam. A few weeks after taking it, I was informed that I had a rare heart condition that had never been detected by my doctors. It only occurs in about one out of every one hundred thousand people, and only really impacts you if you want to be a pilot or an astronaut.

What luck for me.

After working since the age of twelve, and spending all that money and all those years on my education and flight training, I learned that I couldn't fly as a commercial pilot. It was a crushing experience. Imagine nine years of effort taken away because of something you have no control over. The year after that was horrendous.

Not knowing what else to do, I eventually took an entry-level accounting job. It was terrible. For some reason I hadn't translated what I'd learned as an entrepreneur before and during college to my work life after college. I think that happens a lot. The perception in society is that once you get out of school, that's when you get serious and start working at a "real" job.

On the advice of a family friend, I applied to business school. Six months later I got a letter saying I was rejected. Part of the letter said, "If you think this is wrong, you can send a letter back requesting your application to be reconsidered." I called and asked why I was rejected, and they said, "We don't think you have enough work experience."

Now, keep in mind that I had been working since I was twelve, and had spent a year and a half as a pilot prior to interviewing with the airline. So I sent the school a scathing letter. I didn't really expect anything to come of it, but I was upset at life, and upset at the people in the admissions office.

In the letter I said something to the effect of, "You clearly have no idea what it takes to be a pilot! When was the last time your work experience consisted of flying in freezing temperatures, with ice covering the windshield, and you had not only your life, but other people's lives in your hands?" It went on from there.

I didn't expect to hear anything back, and started taking classes to get a degree in education. I figured I would have my summers off and could travel. But three months later, I got a notice from the business school accepting me for the fall. Apparently, someone had received my letter and given things another look.

I entered the night program since I couldn't afford the full-time program. I showed up a few minutes before my first class was supposed to start, and my classmates were all buzzing, something about us being "Number One." I remember thinking, "What's the deal? Number one of what?"

That's when I learned that business schools are ranked, and that the rankings are a big deal. It turned out that I was now a student at the number one business school in the country, which meant that I would be in high demand by top employers when I graduated. I'd had no idea.

To this day, I look at that experience as God, or the universe, handing me one back after what had happened with my aviation career. When I graduated, I was recruited to work as a strategic advisor for companies. It was very lucrative, and I was treated very well.

Five years later, though, I'd had enough. I left it all to go travel around the world.

That led to the first book that was mentioned earlier, and that led me to where I am now; a full-time author and speaker. It's been a strange journey, but in a sense I'm back to where it all began: I'm an entrepreneur again.

Since my first book, I've been inspired to write three others, including one called *How to be Rich and Happy*. It's sort of a tongue-in-cheek title about finding and walking the path to doing whatever you want, whenever you want.

What have you learned from mentors and role models in your life?

Unfortunately, when I was younger I wasn't smart enough, or aware enough, to realize the benefits of mentors. It was only later that I really came to realize how powerful it is to have someone you can learn from. One of the things I now teach is about finding your "Whos." They are the people who are either living, or who have lived, the life you want to live. What I discovered is that life is a heck of a lot easier when you don't have to learn everything on your own. That is what a great Who does for you. Whether they are someone you can talk to directly, or even read about in a book, learning their story is incredibly valuable.

At this point in my life I'm inspired by everyone I come across who has chosen to live life on their terms. I learn something from each of them.

Please share one tip for living a full life:

Discover your Big Five for Life and spend every minute on them! They are the five things you most want to do, see or experience in your lifetime before you die. The five things so powerful that if you get to them, then on your deathbed you'll be able to look back over your life and say, "It doesn't matter what else I did or didn't get to, I got to my Big Five for Life and therefore my life was a success by my own definition of success."

The idea of the Big Five for Life came to me when I was in Africa during my adventure around the planet. It was life-changing for me. It's one of the things I always mention when I'm asked to speak for audiences.

It's a simple concept, and yet it's new for most people. I'll ask an audience of a thousand people how many of them have ever had someone ask what's even one thing they want to do, see, or experience before they die? I'm lucky if a few hands go up.

The thing is though, if we don't start with the end in mind and take the time to figure out what we really want to do with our lives, odds are we won't do it. And that's a shame. Imagine how sad it must be to get to the end of your life and instead of great memories to reflect on, you've only got a bunch of things you wish you would have done.

I won't get into a lot of detail here, but the ultimate is living what I've learned is a Zone Three life. That's when you not only spend your time on your Big Five for Life, you also GET PAID to do, see, and experience them. When I was younger, I never imagined such a thing was possible. Now it seems I meet someone every day who lives that way. It's truly the way to do it.

What would you like your legacy to be?

First and most important for me is being there for my family. Having a great relationship with them is at the top of my own Big Five for Life list.

Beyond that, one of the most humbling, and at the same time rewarding things, has been to receive messages from strangers who have read my books. When someone says, "You changed my life," that's a big statement. I mean, I'm just an average guy, not some kind of guru.

As far back as I can remember I've wanted my life to mean something. If, in addition to having a great relationship with my family, my legacy is that in some small way I made a positive difference, I'll be happy with that.

John's Message:

Discover your Big Five for Life, and spend every minute on them!

ARLEEN BOYD

"Live Aloha."

- Arleen Boyd

Arleen Boyd started her own telecommunications company in the early 1980s after hitting the "glass ceiling" where she'd been working. She enjoyed the cutthroat business world and her CEO status until she realized that she was not running her business: it was running her.

Today, Arleen brings her expertise to companies in the area of social media, building her clients' internet presence to lift awareness, build brands, generate income, and keep customers. She strongly believes in surrounding herself with a network of peers who are also in positions of leadership. This network has allowed her to reach out and collaborate, and to stay grounded. Her philosophy is that allowing yourself to reach out for help in turn allows another person to enjoy the gift of giving.

What inspired you to become an entrepreneur?

I was in telecommunications in the early 1980s when it was just opening up. AT&T was no longer a monopoly, but was broken up into different parts. The company I was working for went through all types of mergers and acquisitions, and eventually I ended up becoming a national account rep for what is now known as Siemens Corporation.

By October of that year, I couldn't work any more because, even though I was paid on commission only, management still put a cap on my income. I was not allowed to make more than the CEO of the company, so I basically had to stop acquiring accounts for them, which struck me as completely ludicrous. I was trying to help the corporate office by showing them ways to acquire even more companies and help the business grow, but they weren't open to it. I decided it was time to do my own thing, so, knowing nothing about business, but thinking I knew a whole lot about telecommunications and marketing, I started my own company in Silicon Valley in 1985.

The company began as what was called an "interconnect" company. We provided business telephone systems and all the things that hooked up to them – like voicemail, call centers, and data networks, as well as local area networks. We expanded that into long-distance networks and ended up with a couple of subsidiaries, which went back to the "big boy" long distance carriers. It was a lot of fun, but it was also a cutthroat, male-dominated industry.

That's how I was initiated as an entrepreneur.

In 1999, I decided I wanted more balance in my life, and decided to sell my company. I went completely online. Today I work with companies, products and people to build their online presence for measured results. A critical wheel on that wagon is social media; one of the spokes in that wheel might be Facebook or Twitter.

What truly inspires me now is being able to help people and businesses take what they have and expand upon it so they can save money, make more money, and give more value at the same time. I was able to do that during the last recession with my telecommunications company: we devised applications for businesses to show them how to utilize what they already had in place to provide better service for their customers while expanding profit margins. In the same way, social media provides an expanded opportunity for cost-effective growth within companies. I build processes and applications for companies and individuals demonstrating how they can give more to their clients, while at the same time earning and saving more. This affects each client's personal economy, which affects their company's economy, which in turns affects their community's economy.

How have you created your life on your terms?

When I became an entrepreneur at the age of twenty five, my

business demanded sixteen-hour days. I remember the year I only took one day off – and that was to have my daughter! Because I was the CEO, I could bring her to work with me (not a course I would recommend to anybody!) but my company was still running me, instead of me running it.

Just because you're an entrepreneur doesn't mean you're living life on your terms. Recognize your purpose, and stay vigilant on that path. What I've found is that you can have it all – you just can't *do* it all at the same time.

While growing my company, I also went through a divorce, and was raising my daughter primarily as a single mom. When 1999 rolled around, I realized it was time to bail from corporate America. I couldn't be the kind of CEO I wanted to be and still be the kind of mom I wanted to be. So I made the choice to sell the company.

I know that not everyone would have made the same choice, and I respect the fact that we are all entitled to our opinions and our choices. I feel fortunate to have had the option to make the choice I did.

Today, as an empty nester, I've made other choices. I've explored new projects and different paths that I would not have been able to choose back when I was a young mother, when I wanted to be the "room mom." Again, it's not that you can't have it all: it's just that you need to make choices about when to have what. When you're learning to live life on your own terms, it helps to acknowledge that you'll have different priorities at different phases of your life. I've learned this the hard way. There was a point in time when I drove myself into the ground trying to be everything and do it all for everybody. That's not healthy: it's just crazy!

What have you learned from mentors and role models in your life?

From a very early age, I read about women in history. People like Amelia Earhart inspired me. Another woman I looked up to, Sandy Kurtzig, was a founder of ASK Computer Systems back in the early 1980s. She provided one of the first models for a self-funding growth strategy for a company in Silicon Valley. I met her a few times at gatherings and community organizations, but I didn't know her personally. Yet, I watched what she did. I studied her. At that time she was outstanding, the only woman I'd heard of who had founded and headed a major technology company.

There have been many women along the way who encouraged me when all I could think was, "Ugh, how can I do this?" Many times, I felt like I was hitting my head against the "old boy" network, so I learned to team up.

Teaming up is key. The methods and practices of our company did not put customers first: the employees came first. After all, how can you take care of your customers unless your employees are top notch? You also need to create a team outside of your employment, a team of peers that you can share with, other people in positions of leadership. Consider networking with organizations that don't necessarily fit together with your own. You might discover a great idea from them, and see how to apply it to your own industry.

A note of conservative caution here: Network with those who are positive in nature. Stay away from those who demean others: they may one day find you a threat and use their influence in a way that creates conflict. Create alliances with leaders who build the merit of others, and give them your support.

Please share one tip for living a full life:

It helps to share responsibilities. There was a time when I was far too independent. At one point, my husband at the time was near death in the hospital. I had a toddler on my hands and a major project with fourteen new employees coming on the next day. I was about to have a meltdown. The Vice President of Pacific Bell (with whom we were contracted) came over to see me, and said, "You simply must pick up the phone and ask for help." I was used to being fiercely independent, but I couldn't go it alone any longer.

There's a difference between interdependency and codependency. Interdependency is a healthy thing: it allows you to give a gift to others. Women in business are often nurturers, but we're so used to giving that we're not very good at receiving. Learn to be a receiver, because receiving allows someone else to feel the joy of giving.

I also believe that women in business need to stand up more, and be stronger for themselves. A very good mentor of mine, the president of a food company, said that I must be shrewd in business. I used to think "shrewd" was a bad thing, but it's really a good thing! Women must learn this: we can be shrewd in business and yet maintain our womanly strength. It's a balance.

What would you like your legacy to be?

For me, thinking in terms of legacy is hard, perhaps because it takes into account the ego. But we need not worry about the ego, so long as we maintain our womanly strength and our attitude of nurturing. Looking at my daughter, who's twenty, and the women of her generation, I think I'd like to leave behind an example that enables them to find the strength in themselves to embrace a balance in life, and to share with and support one another in their endeavors. I'd like to show them that they can give to their families and communities and still nurture themselves. I see too many women today without self-esteem, whose strength is depleted from nurturing others without taking the time to build themselves.

Arleen's Message:

You can be your best self and be fulfilled. Know you are important. Embrace balance.

LORRAINE COHEN

"When we come to the edge of all the light we have and must take a step into the darkness of the unknown, we must believe one of two things. Either we will find something firm to stand on, or we will be taught to fly."

- Patrick Overton

Lorraine Cohen became an entrepreneur because she wanted the freedom to be her own boss, follow her spiritual calling, and make a difference in the world.

Lorraine appreciates that nothing in life is wasted. Every person and experience she has encountered has been of service to her personal growth, spiritual evolution, and business success. To Lorraine, creating life on her own terms means doing whatever it takes to follow the calling of her heart.

What inspired you to become an entrepreneur?

I feel entrepreneurship chose me! As an interfaith Reverend, Doctor, hypnotherapist, and psychotherapist, the freedom to be my own boss, follow my spiritual calling and passions, and make a difference in the world were compelling reasons to start my own counseling practice rather than look for a job. As a soul-based entrepreneur I've had opportunities to help people worldwide positively transform their lives, and to interview incredible people like James Tywman, Neale Donald Walsch, Marci Shimoff and many others.

The people I have worked with have been my greatest teachers, and have helped me become who I am today. As an entrepreneur, the possibilities to create a prosperous and joyful life, while helping others awaken to their destiny, are boundless. I can't imagine doing anything else.

How have you created your life on your terms?

I became more consciously aware in the early 1980s, and began a path of spiritual awakening. Our lives are reflections of who we are on the inside, and to create life on my own terms meant investing time, energy, and an open mind and heart. I had to do the inner work to remember who I was, and what I came here to do and be. Since I learned to follow my inner guidance when making both personal and business decisions, my life has become much more abundant and joyful.

I have also come to appreciate that nothing is wasted. Every person and experience I've encountered has been of service to my personal growth, spiritual evolution, and business success. My life vision is continually unfolding. As a conscious entrepreneur, each time I take my business to the next level, I am stepping into the next and highest version of who I am meant to be. While navigating through the fears, I remember that uncertainty is part of the process of moving forward in faith and trust. Creating life on my own terms means committing to do whatever it takes to follow the calling of my spirit and fulfill my destiny.

What have you learned from mentors and role models in your life?

I have had many coaches and mentors, and have created three mastermind groups in the last eight years.

When I shifted my psychotherapy practice to full-time coaching, I worked with two different coaches who helped me hone my skills and expand my market. This was the third time in my life I had started a new business, and it brought up all of the fears and uncertainty that come with making a big life change. Their guidance and support were invaluable in helping me to resolve pain from the past, clarify my business direction, and take steps to move forward.

The mastermind groups I created have pushed me to raise the bar of small thinking. I've learned what it means to play a bigger game, and the playing field keeps expanding, which is both exciting and scary. Continuing to do the inner work is essential for me to consciously create the life I desire. My mastermind group holds me accountable and keeps me on track with my vision.

My marketing mentor taught me ways to effectively position myself online, from web site setup, to growing my database, creating products and programs, and attracting the right audience to join with me in my business. I also have two other business partners with whom I brainstorm ways to think and play bigger.

Please share one tip for living a full life:

Many years ago I began my own radio program to grow my business and enrich people's lives. I've had the opportunity to have incredible guests on my programs, as well as to be a popular guest and presenter to thousands of people globally. When I receive e-mails from people thanking me for something I said, or when a guest shares something that was meaningful or life-changing for them, my spirit smiles with joy and gratitude.

Be of service to other people's success. Instead of focusing on all the things you want to acquire for yourself – things you think will make you happy and prosperous – turn your focus to ways that you can selflessly and joyfully help others succeed. This might mean gifting your time, energy, money, or advice to enhance other people's lives. It is in the giving that we receive the fullness of life's miracles and blessings.

What would you like your legacy to be?

My passion is helping people to transform fear and limiting beliefs, and awaken to the destiny they have come here to fulfill, both personally and through their businesses. Knowing that I have been a positive guiding light to help people remember who they are; live authentic lives; cultivate faith, courage and love in themselves, others, and the Divine; and bring that love, faith and courage out into the world... That would be a great legacy for me to leave.

Lorraine's Message:

Think and play bigger. Inner work is essential to consciously creating the life you desire. As an entrepreneur, you have the power to create a prosperous and joyful life while being of service to others.

MARIANNE WEIDLEIN

*"Forgiveness, love, and our connection with the Divine is
the medicine that is healing the sickness of our time."*

- Jeremy Roske

Marianne Weidlein initially chose to work for herself because
she wanted to help people in the healing and spiritual arts. She
developed a curriculum for teaching the development of a private
practice, and began offering business courses to the self-employed.
She knows that self-mastery is a key component of success, and in
helping her clients to achieve that goal, she is constantly inspired
to pursue her own personal development.

In 1968, she began living a life on her own terms after dealing
with an abusive boyfriend while she was a single mother with no
other support. She realized that her life was a mess, and activated
herself into a profound motivation to serve in the transformation
of human consciousness.

What inspired you to become an entrepreneur?

I chose self-employment because I wanted a sustainable
connection with a higher power. Working for someone else
makes this challenging and inhibits my creativity. In addition,
I wanted to help people in the healing and spiritual arts to be
successful, because by helping them to reach more people, I could
reach more people than I could on my own. Previously, I'd had
fifteen years in small business management experience, and had
just earned my undergraduate degree in Business Administration,
so I developed a curriculum for designing a successful private
practice, and began offering business courses to the self-employed
and self-employed wannabes.

A few years later, I began doing groups and one-on-one sessions
to help people develop self-mastery and perform at peak levels.
I chose this focus because when I am paid to know something,

I am inspired to excel in it. This necessarily accelerates my development with that focus. As an ex-hippie, like many others of my generation who began changing in the 1960s, I wanted peace, love, and freedom. To gain this, I chose self-mastery, and knew that helping others with this development would require my constant improvement. This was a great plan because it works. Working with clients inspires and motivates me, and between sessions I maintain this self-improvement focus.

How have you created your life on your terms?

I was desperate. I was twenty-four, a divorced mother of a toddler daughter; we were on welfare, and I had no parental or family support. I endured a lengthy and terrifying all-night physical assault by a boyfriend. Soon afterward, he left the state, and I realized that everything about me and my life was a mess. In that epiphany moment, I was activated into a profound, ironclad, and lasting desire to overcome the trials and tribulations of my life, in order to become the very best person I could be, finally feel proud of myself, and feel free. This allegiance motivates me still, and is why I will serve the transformation of human consciousness for as long as I can.

What have you learned from mentors and role models in your life?

My mentors are unusual. I choose them because they inspire and inform me. There are three.

First: scorpions. Odd, I know. But here's why. Initially, scorpions were water animals. Then, when the water receded, some of them figured out how to breathe on land. Unlike us humans, as instinctual beings, they did not feel angry because they weren't getting what they wanted. They didn't feel resentful because it was inconvenient. They didn't blame it on anything or anyone and make them wrong. They didn't feel sorry for themselves because life was so difficult. And from these reactions, they didn't just give up and die, or commit frightful acts against others.

Instead, they figured out how to take in oxygen to survive. I can't begin to grasp how they did this, but indeed they did. At times, when I've felt challenged, I remember the scorpions, and think, "If they did, I will!"

Next come the ancient, giant, and magnificent redwoods. They're very old, and yet they sustain! They sustain because they're all connected. Through one very shallow root system they stay connected and support each other. Plus, I am inspired because in storms they bend in the wind and thus are flexible and resilient.

Lastly, I am inspired by Quan Yin because she embodies the feminine archetype of the Divine Mother. She is merciful, tender, compassionate, loving, protecting, caring, healing, and wise. Many women long to embody these qualities. By developing myself to this high frequency consciousness, I am reminded that I can be my version of resilience like the scorpions and redwoods.

I am inspired by life in its myriad exquisite forms. When something breathtaking happens, something so unusual or precious, I am awed. It captivates my full attention, arouses my heart, mists my eyes in delicious humility to the magnificence of life, and reminds me that life in this challenging world can be grand indeed!

Please share one tip for living a full life:

Develop impeccable integrity. Integrity is defined as the quality or condition of being whole or undivided; completeness. This is important to me for various key reasons.

Being integrous results from my fulfilling my agreements with myself and others, from being discerning in my choices while considering possible consequences, and thereby always being able to rely on and trust myself, in all situations, and at all times. My work has shown me, every time, that at the bottom of every client's deepest issues is an inability to completely trust themselves.

Without integrity and wholeness, we cannot develop and maintain a sustainable success. No one can rely on us. We lose opportunities, resources, money, self-respect and the respect and trust of others. With this, sustainable feelings of security, inner peace, and freedom are mere fantasies. Without integrity, life is sure to be a struggle.

We can unwittingly choose struggle, self-negation, and dysfunctionality and its many consequences. Or, we can choose to care about and love ourselves, fulfill our agreements, and by doing so, endow ourselves with the inner and outer qualities of life that we so deeply want. Honoring our agreements is the key. Plus, this accountability uplifts us to the level of consciousness at which intentional manifestation is easy and rapid.

What would you like your legacy to be?

That I have freed myself from all the conditioned habits that doom me to struggle, pain, and guilt. I have transformed all negative perception, thinking, behavior, and emotions so I embody serenity, complete trust, and joy for being alive every second of every day. This gives me the ability to live my old hippie values that have been upgraded to serenity, integrity, unconditional love, compassion, and freedom. Achieving this state is my reason for being. And in this way, I fulfill my dedication to the planet and to the Divine intelligence that has been with me throughout my life.

Marianne's Message:

Life is full of challenge. You can choose anger and frustration, or you can choose to be resilient and trust that you have the power to change your conditioned mindset and your life.

CHAPTER 2

Self-Discovery

"You have to leave the city of your comfort and go into the wilderness of your intuition. What you'll discover will be wonderful. What you'll discover is yourself."

- Alan Alda

Once you determine that it's time for significant change, you will need to be mindful of your finances and uncover your personal strengths before you begin to lay out your future. A life by design includes healing, creative expression, heartfelt questions, thoughtful answers, and creative brainstorming – and a huge dose of reality.

Scrutinizing your current and future financial scene is part of your discovery process. If you already have a budget in place, this will be a fairly easy exercise. If you are flying by the seat of your pants, you must invest some time to get your finances in order. Before making the leap, be realistic about what you can and cannot do in the short term. Depending on your chosen career path, you may need to apply for a business loan, plan for a minimum of twelve months corporate "combat pay," or both.

My own transition lasted for almost twelve months. Before I was ready to move forward, I had to have several deep and lengthy conversations with my husband, move around some investments, secure a line of credit, negotiate a healthy severance package, and buy a new car. Admittedly, this part of the planning process was uncomfortable for a fly-by-the-seat-of-your-pants woman who'd never thought about money, but I'm glad I went through it: once those things were out of the way, it freed me up to flesh out the other aspects of my business plan. It's hard to dream big if you're worried about where the groceries are going to come from next week!

Even with bare-bones scrutiny, entrepreneurship is always a risk. You will need an uber-dose of courage, a solid yet flexible plan, and unshakable confidence to make it on your own.

While fleshing out your financial reality, it's wise to balance the black-and-white budget data with some creative self-discovery. Reading *The Artist's Way* by Julia Cameron was a big part of my self-discovery process. Years of working in a high-stress environment didn't leave me much room for creative endeavors, and it had been a long time since I'd embraced the deeply creative part of my personality. Ms. Cameron's book provided me with an actionable plan for complete creative recovery and re-discovery, and, along with some intense coaching and meditation, inspired me to reinvent myself and unfold my new calling in a much more abstract and organic way than I ever thought possible. I found the key to unlocking my dormant creativity with stream-of-consciousness journaling, "artist's dates," and weekly discovery exercises.

As a neophyte to the coaching profession with deep ties to the "Old Guard" convention, it seemed natural to color inside the lines while creating the plan for my new business. In the beginning, the logical choice for me seemed to be coaching business owners, general managers, sales managers, and sales executives. After expanding my creative process through the exercises in *The Artist's Way*, however, this notion quickly became unacceptable. Instead, I started thinking big; throwing ideas out into the universe to see what resonated with me. I dreamt of inspiring people to get to know themselves, in the same way I was getting to know myself; to help them be gentle with themselves, live in their bodies, and accelerate living life on their terms. Thankfully, I was able to partner with coaches who taught me how to harness the power of my creativity to complement my business experience and unfiltered personality. I will forever be grateful to Diane Helbig and Deborah Martin for their inspiration, intuition, kindness, and thought-provoking questions.

In the beginning, my inner critic would berate me with statements like: "How could you walk away from eighteen years of sales and leadership success to do this? Reinventing yourself is a waste of time." When I heard that voice I would do my best to think, "Nonsense! Cancel! Clear!" That's a great mental wipe exercise I learned from my friend, inspirational entrepreneur Joe MacQuarrie.

Self-discovery is not just for hippies and philosophers, and involves a whole lot more than taking a groovy acid trip or zoning out to contemplate the meaning of life. As human beings we deserve to uncover our passions, talents and gifts. The self-discovery process enables you to answer key questions about yourself, such as:

- If you could do anything in the world, knowing that you would not fail, what would it be?

- Can you pinpoint the time in your life when you were happiest? What did that look like?

- What do your friends and family members think are your core talents and strengths? How do their opinions differ from your own? Are they seeing something you're not?

- How can you take your true talent and monetize it?

Your individual strengths and interests become your gauge for defining and designing your new life. You get to choose what you do with your time and energy. Steve Jobs summed it up perfectly when he said, "You've got to find what you love."

This is an excerpt from the Commencement address by Steve Jobs, CEO of Apple and of Pixar Animation Studios, delivered on June 12, 2005. This is perhaps one of the most moving speeches I have had the pleasure of reading and viewing. You can find a video of this entire speech on YouTube.

On love and loss...

I was lucky I found what I loved to do early in life. Woz and I started Apple in my parents' garage when I was twenty. We worked hard, and in ten years Apple had grown from just the two of us in a garage into a $2 billion company with over 4,000 employees. We had just released our finest creation, the Macintosh, a year earlier, and I had just turned thirty. And then I got fired.

How can you get fired from a company you started? Well, as Apple grew we hired someone who I thought was very talented to run the company with me, and for the first year or so things went well. But then our visions of the future began to diverge and eventually we had a falling out. When we did, our Board of Directors sided with him. So at thirty, I was out. And very publicly out. What had been the focus of my entire adult life was gone, and it was devastating.

I really didn't know what to do for a few months. I felt that I had let the previous generation of entrepreneurs down – that I had dropped the baton as it was being passed to me. But something slowly began to dawn on me: I still loved what I did. I had been rejected, but I was still in love. And so I decided to start over.

I didn't see it then, but it turned out that getting fired from Apple was the best thing that could have ever happened to me. The heaviness of being successful was replaced by the lightness of being a beginner again, less sure about everything. It freed me to enter one of the most creative periods of my life.

During the next five years, I started a company named NeXT, another company named Pixar, and fell in love with an amazing woman who would become my wife. Pixar went on to create the world's first computer animated feature film, Toy Story, and is now the most successful animation studio in the world. In a remarkable turn of events, Apple bought NeXT, I returned to Apple, and the technology we developed at NeXT is at the heart of Apple's current renaissance.

I'm pretty sure none of this would have happened if I hadn't been fired from Apple. Sometimes life hits you in the head with a brick. Don't lose faith. I'm convinced that the only thing that kept me going was that I loved what I did. You've got to find what you love. And that is as true for your work as it is for your lovers. Your work is going to fill a large part of your life, and the only way to be truly satisfied is to do what you believe is great work. And the only way to do great work is to love what you do. If you haven't found it yet, keep looking. Don't settle. As with all matters of the heart, you'll know when you find it. And, like any great relationship, it just gets better and better as the years roll on. So keep looking until you find it. Don't settle!

Mr. Jobs is one hell of a role model for entrepreneurial passion and persistence. I am grateful to have found this speech online in the midst of my own career transition.

Self-discovery is a blessing for anyone brave enough to inspect their strengths and weaknesses and capitalize on their true nature. Every person in the world is composed of both light and dark, strength and weakness, positive and negative energy, great successes and devastating disappointments. It's what you do with this knowledge, and how you choose to live your life in light of this knowledge, that completes you. You really can do anything you set your mind to do.

Budget crunching and creative recovery are tools to assist you with creating life on your terms. Get clear about who you are internally, outside of the roles you play, and you will begin to discover a delightful and authentic life. Read on to learn more from extraordinary entrepreneurs who redefined themselves and choose to live life on their terms.

APRILLE JANES

"Do one thing every day that scares you."
- Eleanor Roosevelt

Aprille Janes created and led a successful consulting company for ten years. But although her business was healthy and thriving, something was missing: her work was not filled with passion.

An inspiring "unplugged" trip to the Yukon ignited a big change for Aprille. She realized it was time to take off the golden handcuffs and leave her consulting career.

Aprille created a life on her terms by helping women find their authentic voices through inspirational conversation, creative writing, and exercise. Her passion-filled purpose is to teach women how to tune into and nurture their bodies, minds and souls through the creation of new stories and physical activity. Her approach provides women the tools which allow them to show up in the world the way they want to.

What inspired you to become an entrepreneur?

I created my own consulting company, which operated for ten years and worked with companies like Coca-Cola and other big companies in Canada and the U.S., but I discovered it wasn't feeding my soul. I was making their bottom lines fatter and making a big paycheck, but there was something missing. I didn't feel like I was contributing to the world.

I stepped out of the consulting field to claim my dream of becoming a writer. I have had some success there: I have done quite a bit of freelance writing, and have had a couple of short stories published. I moved into teaching and working with writers, and received my certification through the Coaches Training Institute (CTI). Then, I looked around and said, "How do I bring all of this together?"

I've taken my experiences in writing, coaching, and business, and put them all together. Now, I'm working with entrepreneurs, helping them bring the fullness of themselves to their businesses, because I understand that hunger, and their need to feed their bodies, minds, and spirits while they're earning a living.

The catalyst for change was a trip to the Yukon for ten days by myself. I realized that you can get far enough out that you can't distract yourself. There are no radio or TV signals. I had to pay attention to what I wanted at that point. When I did, I came back and registered for the coaching courses. I took off the "golden handcuffs" – what I used to call the consulting job – and stepped out and said, "Whatever the universe brings to me, that's where I'm going to go, because that's where I'm supposed to be."

How have you created your life on your terms?

First, I made the big leap to quit the consulting business. They were willing to work with me, so I went down to working just three days, and still earned more than most people do working full time. But there was something about it that made me feel like I still had a foot in the other world, so I finally said, "That's it, I have to quit." I took the CTI leadership course, and when I completed that, I was ready for certification. What was amazing is that I put out a newsletter to say I needed coaching clients to get certified, and I ended up with ten clients – Bam! Just like that. It was like the universe was saying, "You're headed in the right direction honey, keep going."

Today, I'm leading workshops where people use writing to explore their story. We treat the story as fiction, so they are free to write whatever they want. I share an exercise where you can't tell the difference between fiction and nonfiction. Some people actually write fiction, but most write their truth. We never comment on the writing itself, so you don't have someone up in your grill saying, "I don't know how you could have been treated like that and why didn't you do..." We always treat the characters in the story as just that: characters. This gives the process great objectivity and lets the writers be witnessed. Being witnessed is so powerful. I've had clients who have come out of abusive relationships because their truth is validated. I've had women who have stepped up and claimed their voice because they realized they had something to say that people would listen to. They may have been told all along they weren't worth being listened to. The transition from creating the fat bottom line to letting people reclaim their lives and live bigger – that's what's been really exciting for me.

What have you learned from mentors and role models in your life?

Keep going! We often quit just short of our goals. I've done it too often myself, so I look for a cheerleader who will give me perspective when I've lost my own. For that reason, I have my own life coach and she's an amazing woman. When I can't see the road ahead, her objectivity is invaluable. When I feel like quitting, she makes me check in to see if it's my "gremlin" speaking, or if it's really time to let go.

I've always had a soft spot for Amelia Earhart because she was a woman who lived life on her own terms. She didn't let others' opinions stop her. Her adventurous spirit led her into a man's world, but she maintained her femininity. She's a great role model for any woman. My other hero is Eleanor Roosevelt – again, a woman who created her own path with wisdom and grace. She took whatever life offered, and left her mark on it.

Their lesson for me is to say YES when my intuition nudges me towards something, and see what shows up. I've found my most rewarding and fulfilling roles when I've paid attention to that nudge. You can't figure it out in your head ahead of time. You can only get into action when you get that intuitive hit – which is why we have to tune into ourselves. Amelia and Eleanor were women who heard their inner voice and acted on it. They didn't quit, but trusted that inner urging. That's how they created such an impact in the world.

Please share one tip for living a full life:

You've got to tune into yourself – that means all of you, not just your head. Our bodies never lie to us. When we connect to what we're feeling in our bodies, we'll be on the path to our authentic selves because our heads can't figure it out. That's part of the reason writing is so powerful: women get into their bodies when they're writing. They're not paying attention to what's happening beyond them; they're not editing while they talk or write. When they read it back, the editing hasn't happened, and it becomes more powerful. It really is about tuning into what you're carrying around inside. I sometimes have writers sit on exercise balls when they can't get out of their heads. They become aware of their bodies while they're writing, so they bring all of themselves to the creative process.

What would you like your legacy to be?

That women can show up the way they want to show up. I like knowing that I've helped women let go of the stories that held them back, and that I inspired them to step into their brilliance so they can create the impact they were put on this planet to create.

Aprille's Message:

Your feelings and your story are valid. Embrace where you have been, and then live big. You must nurture mind, body and spirit as you explore your path to success.

Ann Farrell

"Your vision will become clear when you look into your heart."
                                                            - Carl Jung

The moment in which Ann Farrell decided to become an entrepreneur occurred when, approaching thirty years in the corporate world, her definition of success radically changed. She was at the top of her game, and yet she knew that she had to make a significant and risky change, or live forever with the regret of not doing so.

After exploring what she loved most about her corporate career, she realized that her most rewarding moments were those in which she supported others, and enabled them to step up and be their best. Deep down, Ann knew that before she could truly serve others in this way, she must first do it for herself. She took a risk in order to follow her heart, chase her passion, and honor her commitment to family.

What inspired you to become an entrepreneur?

I'll take you back to the moment where I decided to leave corporate life and launch out on my own.

I enjoyed a wonderful, thirty-year corporate career, and was the only woman to have ever worked my way from the bottom to the top of the house in my Fortune 500 Company's one hundred fifty year history. I had the opportunity to execute an executive package, or to stay for six more years to get my full pension. Based on what was going on in my life at the time, the key driver for me was flexibility. I wanted to be able to be there more for my son, who was entering adolescence, and for my father, who was entering the early stages of Alzheimer's disease. My son would soon outgrow after-school programs and my father was fast outgrowing his ability to be on his own. To me, the extra time with them was worth the risk of giving up

43

my executive salary and half of my annual pension to try to make it on my own.

My husband and son know that while I loved my career, I took the risk and made the change because I love my family more than all else. The act of stepping up into my new life was centered in honoring that which is most important to me. It wasn't enough to just tell my family how important they are to me: I had to choose to live it! Taking another corporate opportunity, or continuing in the same job, would not provide me with the level of flexibility that their needs required. Looking at my decision from this perspective, there was only one choice I could have made!

How have you created your life on your terms?

I did exactly what I coach my clients to do! I sat back and asked myself: What are my gifts? What makes my difference and enables my success? What is my voice? What am I passionate about? What are the moments I cherish most when looking back on my thirty-year career? I worked for a truck manufacturer and, candidly, I was always more excited about the people than the products. I thrived on the opportunities I had to support them, and help them see that they were greater than they ever imagined they could be. Throughout my career, I had been helping people, teams and organizations to step up and into their greatness. When I thought about what I wanted to focus on with my own business, it was that. That's what drew me to coaching. My love for, knowledge of, and experience in the corporate world provided me with my perfect niche!

Within six months of launching my own business, its revenues matched my executive salary, and within twelve months, they almost doubled! I drive my son to and from school every day, and have afternoon time with him. I'm also able to support my dad in what is now late stage Alzheimer's. Now, I enjoy success on my terms, and by my own definition!

What have you learned from mentors and role models in your life?

I thank my mentor for teaching me two things: one that I wanted to emulate, and one that I did not.

When I was a middle manager, my work caught the attention of the CEO. He was a tough, critical leader with very high expectations. He paid attention to my achievements, and provided big opportunities for me to do more than I thought I was ready for on several occasions, and through several promotions. He influenced my life in two ways. First, he showed me the power of having someone believe in you more, in critical moments, than you do in yourself. And second, he showed me the risk of letting your work consume your life, since his choices did not necessarily serve his happiness or relationships. Watching him sacrifice big parts of his life over the years only strengthened my resolve to create my life on my own terms.

Please share one tip for living a full life:

For me, the biggest key to living my great life is to love fully. Focus on having it all with passion, not perfection. By staying in the moments and filling them with what I am most passionate about, and by not falling into the trap of perfection, I have created a life that, for me, is rich and fulfilling beyond measure!

To others I would say: "Be true to you!" Create your life on your own terms. Define what success really means to you. Know that your gifts, your passion and the needs that you serve will lead you to your great life and your great work. Your purpose is not one specific thing, like a specific address: it is more like a neighborhood. As you get closer to it, you'll be amazed what you will do, and what will come to you.

What would you like your legacy to be?

I want my legacy to be that I fully loved, and that I inspired others to do the same!

Ann's Message:

Ask yourself: What are my gifts? What need am I passionate about serving? This will take you to the "neighborhood" of your purpose. Therein lies your great life and your great work.

ANNE MERKEL

"I am ... I flow ... I love."

- Anne Merkel

Anne Merkel created life on her own terms through her need to discover and become her authentic self.

The realization that she was not being good to her body sparked a month-long trip to India, which in turn exposed her life as reeling out of control. The autopilot controlled perception of "living the good life" was exposed. Upon returning from India, she profoundly changed her life, completely letting go of everything in her world. After a time of deep introspection, she was able to recreate herself both personally and professionally.

Anne's journey helped her to uncover the importance of trust in your own inherent worth. Her passion lies in supporting others who want to clear out the old stuff that holds them back, but find themselves experiencing pain and trauma around significant change.

What inspired you to become an entrepreneur?

"I feel like I've lived lots of different lives in THIS body."

That's my funny little quote. It means that I've encountered many different life directions and experiences in this lifetime. I've been an entrepreneur since I was a kid, and I've had several different careers. I'm a Boomer that lived Generation X's life. I think that my drive has always been to reconnect with my authentic self and to discover, after wading through and letting go of old patterns and karma, what it really means to live in the internal essence of who I am. I'm continually clearing out the inner and outer baggage in my life so that what's left is an open vessel ready to receive joy, have fun, and live an easy life without struggling to do what I feel passionate about.

How have you created your life on your terms?

My body has been a wonderful guide for me. Whenever I was not going down the right path, my body would fall apart. I had horrible back issues, and was in bed for a year with chronic fatigue syndrome.

Some of us are slower than others to realize that we're in a situation that is not conducive to holistic health. My "ah-ha!" moment came after I had really gotten to know these physical indications about what was and was not good for me. I decided that I wanted to be the clearest channel I could be, and I asked the Universe to bring out the dynamite and clear out all the unnecessary stuff. My mistake was that I forgot to ask for it to be done gently.

So, I went to India. The biggest lesson I learned in my four and one half weeks there was that I was totally out of control in the life I thought I was controlling so well. When I came back, I dove into the process of "thinning out" the life I had been living. On one level – a third-dimensional level – I had thought I was happy. But the soul, the inner passion, wasn't there. That's what was missing. I was in denial. I was married to a wonderful man who was my best friend, lived in a 7,500-square-foot house. I had an established consulting firm which I'd run for years, a full stable of clients paying me lots of money, and a wonderful community of people to play with. But I realized that my old operating process had revolved around using warrior energy to create, and it was wearing me out. Instead of letting life flow to me gently, I was always making it or willing it to happen.

When I returned from India, I ended up getting a divorce, selling my house, closing my consulting business, and moving away from my community to a place where I didn't know anyone. I became a hermit for several years as I went through my own dark night of the soul. When I came out of that, I didn't know who I was anymore; I had done so much inner work that I'd wiped the slate clean. I even had to learn to cook again, because I didn't know what I liked. What I used to cook for my ex-husband tended not to be what I wanted to cook. It was interesting, because although my ex and I were best friends, we were in a codependent relationship: there was part of me that was dependent on him, and he was dependant on me because I was supporting him financially. We ended up being friends again (still are), but we had to get out of that spiral and into a strong healthy relationship where both of us could grow. Not being with him was painful; letting go of my wonderful community was painful, too.

In the years after making these changes, I really recreated who I was and came back into balance. I realized that I am my own divine partner, and I want to have a great time with myself. Whoever else comes along to work with or play with will be icing on the cake. Those discoveries were pivotal for me as I recreated my business and surroundings, and built the wonderful life I have now. Like an artist, you have to start with an empty canvas. I'm still painting, and it's really fun, even though the portrait isn't finished yet.

What have you learned from mentors and role models in your life?

When I see somebody I respect greatly, I try to emulate the characteristics that I most admire about them. And, when I see others succeed in some area, I remind myself that I can easily do that too, if I really want to!

Please share one tip for living a full life:

It's important that you trust that you can create your life for yourself, and that you know you are worthy of living the life of your dreams. If you have any doubts whatsoever, there are wonderful tools you can implement to clear your emotional resistance.

What would you like your legacy to be?

I feel like I've already touched thousands of people worldwide, and was able to improve their lives and work even before I came into true balance myself. I feel like my legacy is helping others who want to clear out the old stuff, but find themselves in a lot of pain and trauma around change. I want to touch those people, and help them recreate their lives. I want them to know that they're not alone – that they've got all the help they ask for – and that it doesn't have to be traumatic to come back into the world.

Anne's Message:

By tapping into your true essence and authentic self, you allow life to flow gently toward you. Embody love and share loving kindness with the Universe and all those around you as you seek your own joy!

DAVA GUTHMILLER

*"Creativity is allowing yourself to make mistakes,
and art is knowing which ones to keep."*

- Scott Adams

Dava Guthmiller grew up in a creative environment filled with entrepreneurial spirit. After several job experiences in which she invested her time working for someone else, she realized she didn't care for the way she, or the clients she interacted with, were being managed. She knew she could do better.

A thriving entrepreneur, Dava has created what she deems the perfect work environment for her staff. She is thrilled that her team members look forward to coming to work every day. Creating award-winning work and witnessing her clients' and employees' successes are what she finds most rewarding.

What inspired you to become an entrepreneur?

I grew up in that kind of environment: my dad was an entrepreneur, and my mom had her own business. I was used to an entrepreneurial mentality.

I came to San Francisco for school, and experienced lots of jobs. The last job I had before striking out on my own was as a senior designer. I was exposed to all sorts of projects, and within two years, I was doing my supervisor's job. It was great that she let me do so much, but there was a lot of tension once it became obvious I was leading beyond her. Although it was difficult, this experience helped me realize I could create a company on my own.

After a couple more years I decided to open my own design firm. I liked the idea that I could be in control of my situation. I didn't care for the way I, or the clients I worked with, had been managed in my prior position, and I knew there was a better way to run a business. I love the idea of discovery, of finding an answer to a problem that somebody else might not have found. With each new client, it's about learning about their business and getting deeply involved. I tend to take on projects because I like the person, or the products they've created. I get to learn their business as well as my own, because I have to be involved in theirs. Creatively, being in San Francisco in particular and bigger cities in general is inspiring: it's the culture, art, and architecture. But I grew up in a small town, so I'm also inspired by nature and community.

How have you created your life on your terms?

I had tried large firms and small firms and I decided that I really wanted to be a smaller company. I like the idea of working with people, instead of having people working for me. I like the team mentality. I like being an owner, and not having a partner or a board of directors to answer to. I like sharing information with my staff.

It took me a long time to hire more than one employee: I had to let go of the control of doing everything myself. But eventually, I hired people who I chose first for their talent, and second for their personality. I make sure each of my employees have a little bit of that entrepreneurial spirit in them – that they want to do more than just sit in a cubicle and be a designer. I surround myself with people who like to work the way I do, and it makes for an awesome work environment.

What have you learned from mentors and role models in your life?

My biggest influence has always been my parents. My dad had two or three businesses while I was growing up, and he was a huge supporter: he let me know I could do anything I wanted to do. My parents were my cheerleaders.

One friend of mine, who I interned with for two years, was also really supportive. The day I quit my job, I called him and said, "What am I going to do?" We met for lunch that day, and a week later I had a name for my business and was sharing an office space with him. He was ten years my senior and a designer doing his own thing. I was grateful to have someone else to bounce ideas off of, and to check in with to make sure I wasn't crazy!

Please share one tip for living a full life:

Share. That word encompasses the way my life has worked out really well. For me, sharing has created the good life. Definitely share your knowledge, whether it's teaching your staff, teaching a class, or giving a lecture. When you do that, you're not only sharing, you're getting back from other people. It's a great way to learn. I actually taught at the Academy of Art University for a couple of years, and it was the fastest way to learn how to work with employees. You need to let go of that control, and teach people how to do something rather than telling them to do it.

Sharing also includes sharing your wealth. We work with two non-profits on a regular basis, donating our design time. I run a woman's networking group that allows me to share my knowledge and my thoughts. Once a year we do a huge event to raise money for a local charity. I also head up the San Francisco chapter of Slow Food. Lots of sharing!

What would you like your legacy to be?

It would be great to have award-winning work out there, and for my clients and employees to be successful. Also, that I created a happy place for people to work.

Dava's Message:

Be willing to learn, and share your knowledge with others. Design and creativity flourish in an environment where everyone supports and teaches one another.

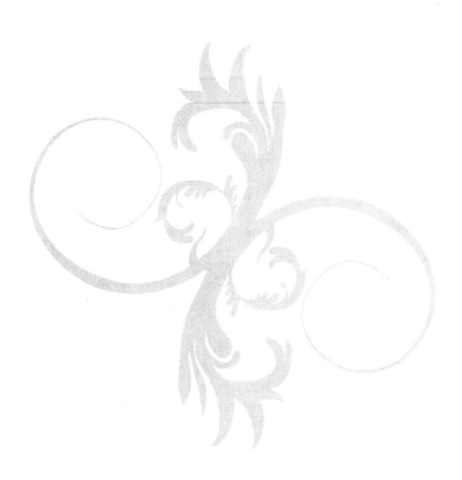

54

CHAPTER 3

Letting Go of Fear

*"You gain strength, courage, and confidence by every experience
in which you really stop to look fear in the face. You must do
the thing which you think you cannot do."*

- Eleanor Roosevelt

Fear is the biggest saboteur of your auspicious goal to reinvent yourself. In order to move past the stage of your initial "I'll do it!" you will probably need to face at least one major fear.

Fears can be like nasty little monsters under your bed, easy to spot and swiftly tamed, or they can be like the lions in a midnight jungle, invisible until the moment they pounce. Either way, they stand in the way of your forward movement, and they need to be overcome – or at least pacified – before you can take the next step toward living life on your own terms.

Fear can take hold of you and cling like an evil shadow until you decide to take action. The voices in your head that mutter things like, "I can't," "I'm afraid," "I'll hurt myself," "I'll let somebody down," "I'm not good enough," or "Don't quit your day job!" represent pesky negative programming that must be undone. If you don't address it, you will continue to play on a fear-breeding mental merry-go-round.

One of the best teachings about fear I've encountered comes from Neale Donald Walsch, who says that FEAR is nothing more than an acronym for False Evidence Appearing Real. How cool is that? We create the fear, we manufacture the monsters in our minds. But if we create our fears, we can also create the mechanisms to overcome them.

If your fears seem too big to tackle, consider itemizing what you are afraid of. Before you take a significant risk (like jumping ship on your unfulfilling corporate job), consider itemizing all of the frightening angles to the best of your ability, and ask yourself, "What's the very worst that could happen?" Acknowledging and accepting the worst-case scenario may be all you need to annihilate your fear and take your first step forward.

When undertaking my own transition, my biggest fear was losing everything I'd created over a lifetime in the broadcast television industry. I had power, money, an exquisite lifestyle and lots of material wealth. How could I chuck the stability to follow my dream? I struggled with severe self-doubt. Was I a fraud? Could I really go it alone?

No matter how you go about it, reinventing yourself can be a manic ride. Here is a poem I wrote while experiencing the mania.

Manic

One day
I rode a manic roller coaster

Twisting and turning
Rising and falling
Crashing through

Frustration
Patience
Hunger
Happiness
Aggression
Love

I prayed for the ride to stop
Yet somehow got off on
The thrill of being out of control

One day
I rode a manic roller coaster

Gaining momentum
Spinning around
Hands in the air

Tangled thoughts
Wanting to climb out of my skin

Inner calm
Understanding how to bask in peace

An endless appetite for life
Contemplating how much is enough

True joy
By appreciating natural riches

Ripping on the way things are
Gaining momentum in my disgust

Kindness and selflessness
Always wanting more
Love . . .

Whatever you want to achieve, know that it can be accomplished with discipline, meaningful play, and imagination. With those tools, you can begin to reprogram your brain to acknowledge and accept new opportunities without all of the negative self-talk.

Awareness of negative self-talk is an excellent place to start building a bridge between who you fear you are and who is really looking back at you in the mirror. Many courageous entrepreneurial souls have come before us, people who have given up everything for a life of personal freedom. There are countless examples, in this book and elsewhere, of men and women who had the courage and the confidence to blaze a trail toward their passion. If even one person can pull this off, why can't you? The process of letting go of fear and making room for great love and passion helps to pave the way to your particular brand of personal freedom.

After thoughtful consideration, much manic behavior, and many soulful conversations, moving toward my dreams became my ONLY option. Coaching, writing and yoga have become the stones that pave my way. Learning to honor my natural rhythm, explore new interests, and inspire others is hugely rewarding. That said, even though I'm immersed in my calling, and chock full of inspiration, contribution and compassion, there are still days when I am overcome by fear. The "Super Shann" days are incredible, but there are other days when I still feel very small. I've learned that it's acceptable to allow yourself to stew in the funk for a while – but then you have to let it go and get back to creation.

> Are your fears grounded in reality, or is your inner critic conjuring them to keep you "safe?"
>
> What is holding you back from creating your life as you wish it to be?
>
> What is the worst case scenario for moving forward on your new path?

On those days when fear gets the best of me, I've learned to let my emotions fly. Storing fear and sadness internally only creates more pain and suffering, so let it all out! It is perfectly acceptable to have a good cry or scream at the top of your lungs. (You might use a pillow to muffle your roar so you don't scare the hell out of the neighbors!)

Spending time in the natural world is another excellent remedy to calm down when you get freaked out. Take a hike along a wooded trail, or go for a walk on the beach. Stepping out of your usual environment and immersing yourself in nature will change your fear-filled perspective. As I edit this chapter I am lounging on the shore of Lake Michigan listening to the waves crash in. What a glorious place to get away from it all!

When everything feels like it's careening out of control, create a list of what is going well in your life. (This is the positive answer to the list of fears you made earlier!) Take a step back and inspect your situation without emotion. Comparing and contrasting what you want with what you don't want is another helpful exercise to let go of fear-based thinking. If you are afraid of something, you must learn all you can about it, and do your best to face the monster, because after all, you created it! Every fear can be overcome with introspection, mindfulness, courage and action. It's only fear of the fear that tells us this isn't so.

In my opinion, fear is highly overrated. You CAN do the things you think you can't do. So take a deep breath, create a meaningful plan, and ask for help with implementation.

All of the entrepreneurs interviewed for this book faced their fears and opened their lives to a bounty of opportunity. Read on to witness the results of their courageous entrepreneurial decisions.

ALICIA CASTILLO HOLLEY

"If you're not part of the solution, you're part of the problem."
- African Proverb

Alicia Castillo Holley created a life on her terms partly out of her need to stand up for herself, and partly out of circumstance. Growing up in socialist Venezuela, Alicia witnessed many less fortunate people trying to escape from extreme situations. Her interest in social work was fueled by her family, who were very active in the community.

For five years prior to coming to America to earn her MBA, Alicia had saved diligently in order to be able to provide a financial cushion for her young family while living abroad – but a financial crisis in Venezuela led to her losing every penny she'd invested just a few weeks before she was due to arrive in the U.S. Inspired to push the envelope, she pressed on with her plans to start a new life for herself and her children. She arrived in Boston, Massachusetts with two kids, two suitcases and two cardboard boxes.

Four months after graduation, Alicia opened Chile's first Centre for Entrepreneurship. During her six-year stay in that country, she formed several companies, including the first privately held seed capital fund. She semi-retired in 2005 and currently lives in Perth, Australia and Houston, Texas. She has become an internationally-recognized speaker and writer.

What inspired you to become an entrepreneur?

I had a good job as a researcher, but my salary was not enough to do what I wanted to do, so I set up a landscaping company. Before that, I had some previous experience as an entrepreneur – I sold cookies and cakes. Not until ten years later, when I decided to get an MBA, did I discover what entrepreneurship really was; the word "entrepreneur" was not even in my vocabulary until I was thirty-five. My first businesses were started by my need to generate more money and my unwillingness to leave science and academia.

Eventually, though, I did leave academia to lead the new product development area of a large joint venture. That's when I started saving money for my MBA.

How have you created your life on your terms?

Part of what led me to create my life on my terms was my desire to stand up for myself, and part of it was circumstance. When I was fourteen, I fell off a horse, and was in a coma for four days. When I came out the coma, I realized that life is such a gift, and that the possibility of death is very real; from that day forward, I embraced my life fully, and decided I was going to make the most of it every single minute. I'm almost fifty now, so there are a lot of extraordinary minutes in there!

When I was thirty-four, I lost all my money after a financial crisis in Venezuela. I had been saving for five years to do a Ph.D., and then decided to get my MBA instead. I was a single mom with two small kids. I had an interview at Harvard, which was the only option I could think of, but I didn't get in. The next year I applied again, better prepared, and received offers for scholarships to three universities. I picked Babson College.

I had everything planned – my savings, permission from my ex-husband, children who were well behaved and could take the adventure – but life showed me a different way. I lost my money, all of it, three weeks before going. Here I was, with two small kids who didn't speak English, and now there's a big financial crisis in my country? I decided I would go anyway. It had taken me a year to get the court to give me permission to take my kids out of the country, I had spent a year working for my community. It was time.

I arrived in Boston with two kids and $1,400. It was a big experience, and we had a great time that first year. We survived our first Boston winter after living in the tropics our whole lives. It could have been a nightmare, but I realized, "I'm making a dream of my life." Once you realize that you can make your dreams happen, you never look back.

What have you learned from mentors and role models in your life?

When I think of my mentors, I particularly remember one of my best friends, an eccentric scientist from Czechoslovakia. She was forty years older than me, and she and her husband lived across the street from us when I was growing up. I remember watching their extravagances from afar. We became friends when I entered the college where she did her research. She was a magical person.

Eventually, I rented a room in her home. I was the only person besides her husband who could stand to be around her because she was so eccentric. She had a car that was decorated like a giant moth. She had a friend that lived with three pumas. She spoke to insects and animals. She also gave me the strength to go hiking in the mountains by myself; before I left, she gave me a bottle of cyanide and said, "You need to learn how to be with yourself in order to be with the world." She taught me a lot of life lessons. My children loved her too. She would come up with the weirdest things: a cube as a wedding gift, a frog for my son, inquisitive questions for all of us.

Each of my mentors have a passion for what they do, and are oblivious to negativity. They enjoy life's challenges, and they always have so much fun!

Please share one tip for living a full life:

The world would be so much better if we all start actively thinking "I have a great life!" Take care of yourself first.

What would you like your legacy to be?

I don't want to put pressure on myself to have a legacy. I am more comfortable with being humble about my legacy and ambitious about my growth. I hope my words can help others find happiness, and I develop programs to create wealth, but my legacy depends on others' needs, and that is completely out of my control.

Alicia's Message:

Find the inspiration in adversity. Make a commitment to improve your situation. Even when the odds are daunting, you're still involved in creating the life of your dreams.

PERRY NIEHAUS

*"If you're going to pull the rug,
make sure you're not standing on it."*

- Perry Niehaus

Perry Niehaus experienced a life-changing moment when he applied for life insurance and was denied. For six days, he didn't know what was wrong, so he began to reflect on what his life represented, and started planning what he would do for the next six months of his life. He figured out where his priorities were, and discovered that he had been living the life of his dreams all along.

What inspired you to become an entrepreneur?

I don't know if I was inspired, or if entrepreneurship was simply a default position. Every time I went to work for somebody else, I always found it necessary to excel beyond what everyone else in the company was doing. Then, I would reach a certain level, and there would be nowhere else for me to go. I really wasn't employable, in the sense that I was a pain in the ass for my employers because I was always pushing the envelope.

I had an interesting experience a short while ago: I applied for life insurance and I was declined. I was under the impression there was something seriously wrong with me. It took six days to get any information from the doctors or the insurance company, so I had six days to reflect on what my life represented. I wondered, "What if I only have six months to live?" I spent those six days planning what I was going to do for the last six months of my life, and I got to figure out where my priorities were. Some people in that position start planning where to travel, and how to do all the things they missed out on in their lives, but I realized that I'd been living the life that I wanted all along! There was nothing left out. Everything I was thinking about revolved around creating an environment where my wife and children and grandchildren could be comfortable for twenty years after I was gone.

I'm the fourth of eight children. My mother was married young and had eight kids in eight years. I grew up on a farm in Alberta. When you're out in sixty-degrees-below-zero weather milking cows and feeding stock, you don't ask why – you ask, "How?" That part of my upbringing was the best, because when I came into the business world, I never had to question if I was going to do something, or if I could do something. When I see something I want to do, I simply ask, "How do I go about doing this?" (On a side note, seven of the eight siblings in my family are entrepreneurs!)

That question – "How?" – has been a major inspiration in my life, and has allowed me to approach everything I do. I can't say there was a turning point in my life where I was inspired: I have simply approached everything I've done with passion and enjoyed it thoroughly.

How have you created your life on your terms?

One of the things I've learned in the last ten years is that the key to life is not knowing the answer. I started my current company sixteen years ago. I sat down at this desk not knowing anything about the industry or the business I was getting into. But I made it work, because I was okay with not knowing – yet.

We live in a day and age where if we ask a question, the answers come to us instantaneously. Spend your time asking yourself, "What is today's question?" When you get the question right, the answer is fairly obvious.

The most exciting part of my business in the last ten years has been learning the right questions to ask every day, and watching the people who work with me grow from those questions. I get as much pleasure from operating my business as I get out of a game of golf, or anything else I do. I can't imagine doing anything else. Sometimes I watch other people struggle because they just haven't figured it out yet, and I have to catch myself, because I want to reach out and tell them, "Wake up, the answer is here! You just haven't formed the question yet!"

What have you learned from mentors and role models in your life?

I was at a big conference in San Diego in 1980, and there were about three thousand people in the room. Then, a guy named Jim Janz walked in one of the back doors, and suddenly everybody in the room knew he was there. He just had that energy about him.

What I learned from that situation is to live life large enough that people want to be around you. I learned to live my life in such a way. People don't know what I have, but they know they want some of it. On that day in 1980, I decided that nobody will ever forget me. When I leave the room people will either smile or spit – but both are better than being forgotten.

Please share one tip for living a full life:

When I was a teenager, my parents had very few rules for me. On Friday night, my dad's rule was that I could do anything I wanted, so long as I understood I would be in the barn at 5:30 a.m. milking the cows. "If you want to go out on Friday night and stay out until 4:00 a.m., that's fine," he'd say, "just remember you'll be putting in a fourteen-hour day on Saturday."

When I was fifteen, I did just that. At 9:30 the next morning, I was on the way to my neighbor's farm to pick up a piece of equipment for the tractor, and I fell asleep while driving. I woke up as I was flying down into a ditch, and could only watch as the twelve-thousand-pound tractor came down on top of me. In that instant, I was in complete surrender, and I accepted the fact that my life was over. Those few seconds (which felt like three hours) were the most peaceful, calm, and relaxing I had ever experienced, because I came to understand that there is nothing to fear.

When you come to understand that there is nothing to fear, life will progress. Everything that happens in our lives that hurts us or holds us back is based on fear. When we can completely give up our fear, we can do anything.

LIFE ON YOUR TERMS

What would you like your legacy to be?

I want to live my life in such a way that people are attracted to the way I live, and want to find out what I have so they can have some of it too. I hope this will lead them to ask their own questions, and find their own answers.

Perry's Message:

If you're asking yourself the right questions, the right answers will inevitably come to you. Don't focus on fear, death, or the impossible: they're all figments of your imagination. Give up your fear, claim your life, and live it to the fullest.

LISA VINTON

"Every decision you make affects the rest of your life."
                                                    - Lisa Vinton

Lisa Vinton was entrepreneurial-minded even as a young child. She has always had a need to put other people first. At the age of twenty-four, while raising two children, she started a secretarial service, Services for Success, with very little knowledge about running a business.

On her fortieth birthday, her father was diagnosed with cancer, so she quit her job and made her father her priority. Before he passed away, he told Lisa to re-launch Services for Success and take it to the next level. She did, and the rest is history.

What inspired you to become an entrepreneur?

Since I was a child, something inside of me compelled me to help people. When I was eleven years old, I decided to raise money for the March of Dimes twenty-mile Walk-a-Thon, even though I didn't know anyone who was a recipient of those funds. I went around the neighborhood and collected ten cents here, a dollar there. I was exhilarated, and shared my experience with everyone. From that moment on, everything changed for me.

In 1990, when I was twenty-four, I started my own business, a secretarial service typing real estate appraisals. I saw a huge need for other small secretarial services to form an alliance, so I started a local group called Professional Secretarial Network, even though I knew nothing about directing a working group!

A few years later, I got a divorce, sold my business to another woman in the group, and went back into the workforce as an administrative assistant at a new engineering firm. Even in the midst of a recession, it was an amazing opportunity, and within twelve years I had earned my way up the ladder to Chief Operating

Officer. At that point, I realized I had my life back together, and that it was time to start doing what I really loved, which was giving back to other people.

When my father was diagnosed with cancer in July 2005, I decided to resign from my job and make my father my priority. He died six months later. Before we learned that he was terminal, I told him I didn't want to go back to work, that I wanted to have a career that would allow me to be with him. He suggested that I re-launch Services for Success and take it to the next level by helping small businesses.

About a week after my dad died, I had lunch with a girlfriend who told me that her husband was leaving his job to start his own firm, and that he wanted me to help. In two weeks, we had his business up and running, and in his first nine months he grossed nearly one million dollars! I was so excited to realize that I could actually do this! Within five months, I was helping the local dog groomer, a chiropractor, an accountant, and many more people who wanted to grow their businesses in our fabulous community.

How have you created your life on your terms?

I think of myself as a pioneer of my own life. I know no boundaries, other than those that I have intentionally created for myself – ensuring that I maintain my integrity and character, and that I take personal responsibility for my choices and actions. I live a life of "firsts," reaching deep into my soul to find my purpose in life, and I don't allow others to dictate to me what I can and cannot do.

What have you learned from mentors and role models in your life?

I did not have a mentor until I was twenty-eight years old. He was the owner of the engineering firm where I worked for more than twelve years, and he taught me more about business than I learned in school and from any other employer. He taught me about character, integrity, dedication, communication, and commitment. He even taught me how to be a better parent! But most of all, he taught me to believe in myself; that I am worthy!

Please share one tip for living a full life:

Believe in yourself, and trust your inner voice. Put other people first. Serve those around you. Through self-awareness, you can grow as a person and work toward fulfilling your life's purpose.

What would you like your legacy to be?

I would like my legacy to be that I recognized the gifts with which I was blessed, and that I unselfishly used them to help others.

Lisa's Message:

We can create an amazing life with determination and the support of our loved ones and community. Taking time to contribute to the lives of others adds a sense of enjoyment and fulfillment in your own life.

STACIE TAMAKI

"What would you attempt to do if you knew you could not fail?"
- Dr. Robert Schuller

When Stacie Tamaki's business first came to life, she didn't realize she had become an entrepreneur. A friend invited her to create some custom couture veils for a bridal fashion show. The veils were a tremendous hit, and catapulted Stacie into an exclusive and successful niche within the bridal industry.

Stacie is inspired by being open to a wealth of opportunities, making others happy, and cultivating new experiences. She created life on her own terms by believing that she can do anything. Of course, there have been things she tried and couldn't do – but the point is, she tried! Even failure is confirmation that she practices what she preaches, and keeps her conscious about seizing new opportunities.

What inspired you to become an entrepreneur?

In college, I was an advertising art major, but I dropped out a few months before graduation. I spent the next decade working in retail sales, first at The Limited and then at Nordstrom. I had no idea at the time that both of these experiences would make me a more effective entrepreneur – but not only did I eventually become my own graphic designer, my understanding of merchandising, sales, and customer service help me every day in my business.

In 1997, my friend Wendy recommended me to create some veils for a bridal fashion show. I said yes, even though I didn't know how to make them. I went to the craft store, bought a pattern, and made six veils. A few days after the show, the bridal boutique contacted me because people wanted to order custom veils for their weddings. I soon realized I had an undiscovered talent for creating custom couture veils, delicate bridal hair accessories, and matching jewelry. Once I understood that the opportunity before me was something I could turn into a business, I went with it. People were paying me to do something fun!

At the time, I was clueless about what it meant to be an entrepreneur. When people ask me now what it was like starting out, I have to laugh. I was blissfully ignorant about how much work was involved in creating a successful business. I tell people now that I probably wouldn't have gone through with it had I known what it would take – but by the time I understood the depth and scope of what I'd gotten myself into, and all the time and energy it would take, I was so far into the process that I didn't want to back out. And that's how The Flirty Bride came into being.

Later, I taught myself how to build my own web site from a book. To my amazement, people immediately wanted to hire me to redesign their web sites. Even as I told my clients that I didn't really know what I was doing, demand for my services continued to grow. I spent a few years simultaneously designing custom bridal accessories and developing custom web sites for other small business owners. At the same time, I was searching for the perfect online wedding resource to advertise my bridal accessories. As my expertise as a web designer/developer grew, I realized that I needed to create the online resource I had been searching for – and that I now knew how to do it. It was at that point that my focus changed.

The Flirty Guide is the result of the first intentional business decision I had ever made. I saw a need, and created a company to fill it. The Flirty Guide is an online wedding and event planning resource that presents unique wedding ideas to brides and grooms, and offers advertising to a very short list of talented, nice, and trustworthy event industry professionals. The best part about creating The Flirty Guide was that I created short- and long-term business plans, and am now following the path I created with people I respect. Does it get any better than that?

How have you created your life on your terms?

When I approach new situations, opportunities, and ideas, it's with the belief that anything is possible. If I don't know how to do something, I can learn, and if I'm willing to work hard enough, professionally or personally, I can accomplish anything. If I try and fail, that's okay too: failure simply means I challenged my perceived limitations, took a chance, and was open to yet another opportunity.

What have you learned from mentors and role models in your life?

When I was developing my bridal accessory company, I watched *Oprah* every day and *The Good Life* on HGTV every week. I read *Victoria* magazine, and immersed myself in the stories of others who had taken a risk and created something special. Some of the people on *The Good Life* gave up very stable professions to pursue a dream. Some, like designer Tracy Porter, became wildly successful, while others were living paycheck to paycheck, but ultimately all of them were more content with their lives.

In my opinion, there is no faster way to learn how to improve your company than to learn how to separate your emotions from your business. Ask for and embrace constructive criticism from people whose opinions you respect. One of my first mentors, Christine, taught me not to do what was easy, or even what clients were willing to accept. She taught me to always uphold quality as my first priority. By sharing this one piece of constructive criticism with me, she laid the foundation for every business endeavor I would undertake from that point forward. My online resource, The Flirty Guide, is about honoring and elevating colleagues who feel the same way by only allowing those with a similar business philosophy to become advertisers.

Years later, I heard about SCORE (Service Corps of Retired Executives). When I met John, a counselor at SCORE, he said "I can't understand why you're not fabulously wealthy." I laughed and said, "Neither can I!" He took me under his wing and taught me more about being an entrepreneur. It was John who realized that I wasn't comfortable with money – from my perspective, money often brings more misery than happiness – but one day, he finally found the way to motivate me. He knew I had a soft spot for helping others, and pointed out that if I made lots of money, I could become a philanthropist and start a foundation of my own.

That was all I needed to hear. In my spare time, I've started a web site called MarrowDrives.org, which teaches patients how to launch a lifesaving bone marrow donor drive, and recruits potential bone marrow donors to help save one of the thousands of patients in need.

Please share one tip for living a full life:

My favorite quote, from Dr. Robert Schuller: "What would you attempt to do if you knew you could not fail?"

Failure isn't something to be ashamed of. Every day there are small choices that can change where you're going and what you are accomplishing. If you ignore opportunities because you're afraid to fail, you'll stay exactly where you are. For those who are content, that's fine, but I know there are a lot of people that would be happier if they could work at a job they love, be with a person who respects and supports them, or live somewhere that suits them more than where they currently live. For them, change would be good – but the only way to create change is to take chances.

What would you like your legacy to be?

I want people to follow my example and pursue what will make them happy, and do it in an honorable way. In the big scheme of things, what you do isn't just about yourself. How you choose to live your life can and does affect others and their ability to achieve their own happiness. Live and give with kindness in your heart, and it will come back to you.

Stacie's Message:

Opportunity is all around you, and it's yours for the taking. Embrace it, and don't let fear of failure stop you from living the life that fulfills you!

CHAPTER 4

Graceful Transitions

"Discovering your groove and creating a luscious life is all about allowing for grace through your next transition."

\- Shann Vander Leek

You have made the choice to change your life, and you've faced off with (or at least identified and growled at) the gremlins of your fears. Now, it's time to begin your transition. This chapter will guide you through the four stages of the transition cycle, and provide strategies to help you move gracefully through each moment of the experience.

Deborah Martin, my mentor and coach (and one of the extraordinary entrepreneurs in this book), shared the following information with me when she learned that I planned to follow in her footsteps and become a professional transition coach. It is with pleasure that we pass this teaching on to you.

The first stage of any significant transition begins with suffering and skin-crawling discomfort. You know a radical change is coming, but you might not be sure what to do about it. Chances are you will be down in the dumps. You may feel frightened, angry, uncertain, or like you're reeling out of control. I remember feeling lost in a fog, and completely freaked out by the fact that the ideals of the corporate broadcast sales business model – the ideals around which my whole former life had been built – were no longer acceptable.

For some the biggest battle against fear also happens here – after the decision to create change has been made. You might feel as though you've jumped in headfirst, only to discover that you can't swim. (If this is the case, try working with the exercises in Chapter 3 before you start back-paddling.)

During this painful first stage, I recommend staying with your regular, comfortable routines. When you are filled with a black hole of uncertainty, the best thing you can do is create a nurturing daily plan focused on self-care. Try to cut back on extraneous commitments at home or work, and take the time to be gentle with yourself.

Items on your daily to-do list might include: inspirational reading, watching a magical sunset, choosing fresh-cut flowers for your desk or dining room table, playing on a swing-set, soaking in a hot bath, listening to great music, practicing yoga or Tai Chi, playing outside with your family, preparing a healthy meal, or writing in a gratitude journal. Joyful activities like these help to balance the stress and suffering.

But while you're nurturing yourself through your discomfort, remember that nurturing is not running away. Look at yourself in the mirror, and be honest about what's happening inside. Accept the fact that you're suffering, but don't accept that your suffering is permanent. Ask yourself what really separates where you are from where you want to be. Honesty is key to healing and flowing through a monumental change.

The second stage of transition involves deep introspection. You may start to withdraw from the world, retreating into a safe and private emotional space. Initially, this might be a way to protect yourself from the pain and uncertainty you're feeling, but this retreat can also allow you to begin to let go of old patterns and behaviors which stand in the way of your positive transition. You may feel contemplative, curious, spiritual, detached, or highly emotional – sometimes all at the same time.

Writing your thoughts in a journal is a good activity to try at this stage, especially if you're feeling withdrawn and are having trouble talking to the people around you. If you're still unclear about where you're really going, try making a simple compare/contrast chart. Fold a piece of paper in half, and label one column "Want," and the other "Don't want." Then, fill in the blanks. Knowing what you don't want is just as important as knowing what you do. It helps you set boundaries and build a solid foundation for your ideas.

Another helpful suggestion is to spend time in nature, soaking up the beauty of your surroundings. Plan to take a walk along the beach, hike in the woods, or visit a local park. Allow yourself plenty of time to heal from the pain and anguish of the first transitional stage. During my own time of introspection, I scheduled as many lunches as possible at a local park on the shores of Lake Michigan. Stepping out of the office and being quiet for even thirty minutes helped me stay on my path, and being close to the water kept me grounded.

Remember that the second stage of transition is about healing and nurturing your mind, body and soul, but it's also a time for examination. Find the activities that keep you focused, not distracted, and don't be afraid of the deep work. Becoming who you really are means surrendering to change.

The third stage of transition is a big shift from the first two. It's filled with positive energy and includes research and exploration in the outer world. When you reach this stage, you are finally starting to feel like you have some direction. You've gotten an inkling of what the real nature of your upcoming transition might be. You are ready and eager to move forward, and curious about all the new possibilities. You become secure, optimistic, and confident. You are uncovering a new path and ready to walk through the doors of a ripe new opportunity. In this stage you will want to explore the Internet, read about new topics of interest, and continue to write in your journal.

If you are struggling to identify and clarify your interests, consider using a mind map. Sometimes, this simple tool can be just the thing to help you uncover the hidden gems of your future. Wikipedia says, "A mind map is a diagram used to represent words, ideas, tasks, or other items linked to and arranged around a central key word or idea. Mind maps are used to generate, visualize, structure, and classify ideas, as well as aid in study, organization, problem solving, decision making, and writing." (www.wikipedia.org)

To me, mind mapping is simply a creative visual twist on brainstorming. The first time I played with this technique, it blew my mind wide open: what a powerful way to cultivate your ideas!

To create your own mind map, pick up a poster board and draw a large circle in the center of the page. Write your central idea or concept in the circle, and write your supporting ideas around the outer edge of the circle, so that they're linked to the central idea (perhaps jutting out like the rays of the Sun). Expand from there.

You can use mind maps to explore all kinds of creative notions. If you prefer to create your masterpiece online, there are some great mind mapping web sites out there. I recommend Mind Node or Mind42.com.

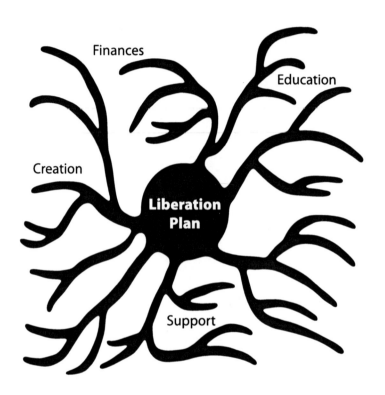

Your discovery period is also the perfect time to explore new connections and talk with trusted confidants. Immerse yourself in discovery – not just in your chosen field, but in any area that interests you. Sometimes, even things that are unrelated on the surface can work themselves into your new path in unexpected ways. Allow yourself to play on a brand new playground!

When you have navigated the first three stages – fear and discomfort, going internal, and exploring new frontiers – you are ready to move into the stage of creative renewal.

The fourth stage of transition is a blast. When you reach the creative renewal phase, your vision has become clear, and you're ready at last to create life on your terms. You are highly energized, committed, and optimistic. You are also determined to make significant changes quickly. Things seem to flow quite naturally for you. Mentally and physically, you feel unstoppable, because you know that everything is possible.

When you experience your creative renewal, allow yourself to be in the flow of the moment. Allow your plans to unfold without force. Become enamored of your new path, hang loose, and enjoy the magic carpet ride! I declared my new path on New Years Eve while surrounded by my friends and family. What an exciting time to acknowledge and embrace my future and let go of all the uncertainty and discomfort!

Each stage of a significant transition can last from a few weeks to several months. Honoring and caring for yourself, and allowing the process to unfold naturally, will help you move through the difficult stages of transition quickly.

1. What stage of transition are you experiencing right now?

2. How long have you been in this stage?

3. What do you need to do right now to honor the stage you are experiencing?

I have navigated the choppy waters of an enormous career transition, and have successfully reinvented myself – but I couldn't have done it without the love and support of my family, friends, and a couple of world-class coaches. No matter what stage of transition you're in, don't be afraid to reach out for help. You don't have to go through it alone!

Next, four more inspirational entrepreneurs share their stories of transition and courage.

DEBORAH MARTIN

*"Sometimes I believe as many as six
impossible things before breakfast."*

- Lewis Carroll

Deborah Martin describes herself as a big dreamer, irreverent and quite lazy. In her opinion, those are all the things you need to be a successful entrepreneur. After working a series of jobs where she didn't fit in, and having invested a great deal of energy trying to "fix" the things conventional wisdom said were wrong with her, she decided to create her own business. Coaching has allowed her to be all of the things she once thought were negative, and thrive in her own authenticity.

What inspired you to become an entrepreneur?

I'm an easily distracted person with a huge dose of irreverence. I'm a big dreamer. And ultimately, I'm pretty darn lazy. In my opinion, each of these behaviors play to being an entrepreneur.

I'm a child of the 1960s, and my irreverence developed about that time. Growing up, the number one complaint on my report cards was "She daydreams too much, and is lazy." I'm also a highly sensitive person in that I tend to be incredibly intuitive, even to the point of being an empath; however, I've never desired to pursue that empathic side of myself, because my irreverence stops me. The beauty of being truly irreverent is that you can also turn that irreverence back on yourself.

I'm not sure what in particular inspired me to live life on my own terms. I just knew I didn't fit. For the first part of my life, I saw my daydreaming and laziness and irreverence as negative, and tried to "fix" them. I didn't do a very good job of it. My discomfort carried over to careers and jobs, and I never stayed with anything very long. I opened my first business in 1983 because I just got tired of not fitting. While I actually enjoyed jumping from job to job, the leaving was always painful because there was a lot of trauma and drama around it – I'd get fired, or somebody would feel compelled to push me out the door, even in a gentle way, because I was threatening to them or the system in which they worked. This pattern drove me to create life on my own terms. I didn't get inspired until much later.

How have you created your life on your terms?

When I became more entrepreneurial, and could do things on my terms. I realized that there were people who actually admired my irreverence and daydreaming, and the fact that I was lazy and highly opinionated. People actually wanted to pay money for my authenticity, which tickled me pink. I got to take the things I had been trying to fix all my life and leverage them. That was inspiring for me.

I started consulting because I had no idea what coaching was – and via consulting, in 1995, I discovered coaching. Everything fit! I could be a daydreamer and I could be lazy. I could be opinionated and irreverent. If people wanted to work with me because of me, great! And if they didn't, that was okay, too. Things just got easy.

I want to play, and fish, and trust that life is going to take care of me because I'm doing what I love to do. A lot of it has to do with knowing that whatever I want to have, whatever I dream of – even if mechanically it appears impossible – it's very possible. If there's somebody who's going to pay me good money for my opinion or my coaching, there's also going to be someone who's going to pay me for playing and fishing. It's not my job to figure out how that's going to happen.

What have you learned from mentors and role models in your life?

My mother taught me to have an opinion, perhaps to an extreme. I have opinions on just about anything, and love them. She also taught me to be polite, so I learned to share my opinions as just that: opinions. I don't have any attachment as to whether someone takes my opinion and does anything with it. I try to avoid giving advice, which to me has an attachment, and maybe even an arrogant component – but I'm happy to share my opinion.

My friend Susan and Coach Thomas Leonard taught me to be curious. In my twenties, I was so amazed and impressed with the bold questions Susan dared to ask, and not only get away with, but be appreciated for. She taught me it's not what you ask, it's how you ask it. With this model to follow, I no longer had to curb my curiosity about others. I started following her lead. When I was in my forties, Thomas taught me to hone my curiosity in a way that got to the heart of matters much more quickly. My coaching soared with this new skill.

My father taught me to fish. I've far surpassed him in that arena because for him it was a hobby, but for me it has become a passion. Through his example, and his desire to spend time in a boat with me, I learned a lot about fishing – and, just as importantly, I learned a lot about relishing the mystery without trying to solve it, letting go, being patient, being present, appreciating that which is elusive, and being vulnerable in nature's elements without fear. The insights one arrives at while sitting in a boat, being still, and waiting for your desire to present itself, amaze me.

Please share one tip for living a full life:

Irreverence and sensitivity were the things I had to embrace and enjoy about myself, and learn to flaunt. Once I quit thinking of them as barriers, they weren't in my way anymore. Instead of taking on your adversary, learn to align yourself with your adversary: then, there is no adversary.

I have big dreams, but I don't turn them into goals. I think goals are where a lot of folks trip themselves up, because they were taught in school to turn their dreams into goals. We break our dreams down into goals, which have strategies, and then we break our strategies into action steps, and our dreams become all about doing. I learned early on that it wasn't necessary to create goals from dreams; I'm lazy, so I don't want to do that. Things are much more effortless if I don't take my big dreams and break them down.

It's not always easy for me to inspire people to go after their dreams without goals. I think it's counterintuitive for people to "take steps" toward their dreams and concern themselves with how it's going to work out. Really, the biggest step for most people is stepping back. (Michael Losier calls it "removing doubt," Deepak Chopra calls it "allowing the Universe to handle the details.") Hang onto your dream without minimizing or diminishing it, without reducing it to something less than what it is.

What would you like your legacy to be?

I love this question! My answer is: I don't care! I say it in my newsletter all the time: "Take what works for you and leave the rest, I won't mind a bit." That's the way I feel about legacies.

It will be interesting to see what my legacy is when I'm gone, if I leave one at all. I sure don't want to figure out what it is now, and I don't want it to dictate my actions. Like a goal, a legacy would direct me in ways I don't want to go, or I might shift away from something a lot quicker because I was attached to the idea of a legacy. I think folks with kids might have a different answer to this question, but for me, in terms of a worldly legacy, I just tell people to have a good time talking about me when I'm gone.

Deborah's Message:

Are the so-called negatives about you genuinely negative? Remove your personality "barriers" by embracing them. Accept and honor yourself and the way you flow. Your career choices, creativity and spirit will open up when you stop trying to make yourself fit into systems that don't nurture your natural patterns. Keep your dreams colorful and big, and go after the impossible!

Jim Blaha

"We've got 6.7 billion people in the world, no two are alike, no one is perfect, but yet we are all perfectly human."

- Jim Blaha

Jim Blaha believes that "The unexamined life is not worth living" (Socrates). He encourages everyone to do all they can to appreciate their education, experiences, and efforts, and live their best life.

What inspired you to become an entrepreneur?

After twenty-five years as an executive with Westinghouse, I asked myself: "Is this what I want to do for the rest of my life?" The answer was "NO!" Shortly afterward, I resigned, even though I had three boys in college at the time. All on my own, I bought into an investment bank. There were only two of us: myself and the founder. It was completely different than what I had done with Westinghouse and I welcomed the change.

I'm a believer in "male menopause," or midlife crisis: it was at that time in my life when I started asking myself if what I had was what I really wanted. Westinghouse had been very good to me, but even though I was top management in my division, I still felt like an employee. Now I've made the break, and I'm doing what I do as an individual. That makes a big difference in how you get out of bed in the morning, and the decisions you make in your day.

How have you created your life on your terms?

At the time I left Westinghouse, the company was going to transfer the bulk of their operations to Fayetteville, NC, where they were building a new plant. I knew if I stayed with them I would have to relocate again, and I had already done that four or five times. My wife and I decided that we wanted to stay where we were, and let our boys attend the same school system.

What have you learned from mentors and role models in your life?

I make a distinction between mentors and coaches. Sometimes mentors are not always obvious, but coaches are an obvious one-on-one relationship. I had mentors in higher positions throughout my career, but the two mentors I go back to are my father and father-in-law.

My father was a blue-collar worker in a foundry. Until I was six years old, we lived in Cicero, Illinois, one of the most bigoted cities in the country. Despite the atmosphere, my father respected all people as human beings, and I learned to not be judgmental.

When I met my wife, I moved from a blue-collar family to what I considered an "upper-end" family. My father-in-law was one of the longest-serving circuit court judges in Illinois. One Thanksgiving, we were the last two left at the table, and I asked him to share some of the important things that had made a difference in his life. He had four answers: three were literary, and the fourth was more unusual. The books were *Huckleberry Finn* and the other Tom Sawyer books, works by Horatio Alger, and *The Prince and the Pauper.* The fourth was a psychological study that attempted to answer the question of love versus survival.

Please share one tip for living a full life:

This question directly relates to the theme of my next book, *Know Thyself: The Unexamined Life Is Not Worth Living.* In my book, I make distinctions between the "whole life" and the "full life." A whole life is birth to death, whereas a full life takes that flat line and puts big cycles and ups and down on it. For example, within six months of graduating from Northwestern University, I was hired at a corporation and got engaged to my wife; those were the "up" times. But the following December, when the wedding invitations were to be mailed out, I had a major breakdown. I called it the "Crash of 1959." But it played an important part in helping me discover the key to the good life – a full life.

What would you like your legacy to be?

It starts with the idea of "know thyself." Everyone should keep some type of journal. I gave my granddaughter a journal about four years ago. Now, she's fourteen. Recently, she had a dance to go to, and I asked if she would journal about it; she wasn't sure if she would. I told her, "These are the times you'll want to remember in ten years."

Your legacy is what you pass on. The best legacy you can leave is the certainty that you have lived your best life, and that you have helped other people to realize that they need to ask themselves, "Who am I? Who do other people think I am?"

Jim's Message:

Embracing the ups and downs of life gives you a greater appreciation of where you are and where you're headed. These cycles are all part of a full, rewarding life.

ILHAM SHEBANI

"To be or not to be, that is the question."

- Shakespeare

Ilham Shebani was inspired at a young age to dedicate her life to improving herself and the lives of others. She pursued and completed several university degrees as a young woman, but felt she was not really applying her education or using it effectively in her career development. At one point, her career was lagging so far behind her education that friends and family started asking when she was going to get a proper job.

Though she had accomplished a great deal, Ilham was unfulfilled in her work, and felt stifled by her employers. At the age of twenty-four, she started her own business. Today, she's creating a collaboration movement that she refers to as a "business revolution."

What inspired you to become an entrepreneur?

My father has had a major influence on my path to becoming an entrepreneur because he made a point of always encouraging his daughters to pursue their dreams, work for the benefit of society, and be prepared for the future. He did this by taking the bold step to move to London, UK after taking up senior government posts, graduating from the military, and completing his law degree while serving as the Libyan Ambassador to Morocco and Somalia.

While we attended private summer schools in the UK, my father continued to invest in our primary, secondary and university education. I was an exception to this rule because I went to a comprehensive school in London. I attended a British university to study political sciences, and completed a BA with honors and a Master's in International Relations within the same year at two universities in London without asking my father for a single penny. Why? Because I wanted to do it on my own, prove that I could stand my own ground, and set myself apart from other members of the family. I worked part-time in sales and volunteered with Amnesty International while completing my studies. It was a tough challenge, but I was very determined, and managed to gain the support of my university director and my family, who knew that my quest for knowledge would provide me with the foundation for personal growth.

I loved the "intellectual buzz" of working, living and studying in London academic circles, but this took me too far off-center. I started accumulating knowledge but not really applying it or using it effectively in my career development, so my career was lagging behind to the point where friends and family were asking when I was going to get a "proper" job. I went to recruitment open days, but recruiters thought I was over-qualified, or didn't fit their ideal candidate profile. I wasn't really sure what I wanted, either, so I began to do a further course on teaching, education and management to become an adult trainer.

Again, my employer found me to be "different" because I kept asking my department manager if I could introduce a training program for my students to develop their personal development and career-related skills; he agreed, and was very supportive. I then organized a recruitment open day at the end of my course so my students could meet potential employers in their field of expertise (these students were training to be interpreters in the community). Again, I did all this of my own initiative, and I worked many extra hours to put my ideas into practice. Within a short space of time, I did so much at my part-time teaching job, Sunday sales job, volunteer work with Amnesty International, and as a student Ambassador during my university studies that when I went for interviews, employers questioned how I could do all of this at the same time! And, I had managed to complete a BA and a Master's degree at the same time? They must have thought I was either mad or lying!

Even though I achieved so much in a short space of time, I still wasn't satisfied. I was unfulfilled. I was misunderstood and under-employed. Most employers expect you to do your job, and that's it! There were no chances for innovation, creativity, promotion, or bigger projects where I could utilize all my skills and abilities.

I decided to take an aptitude test which revealed my strengths, weaknesses, and opportunities in terms of my career potential. I realized that I am an entrepreneur and an advocate for the underprivileged to the core!

I was twenty-two when the light bulb switched on and I started to think about what sort of business I wanted to start. I was living in London at the time, and had already completed my Master's, so I enrolled on a business start-up training course by In Biz Co. I prepared an outline of my business plan, but when my business advisor met with me, he said, "You are too academic. You lack business experience."

Shortly after that, I got engaged, and was married within a month. I became pregnant and everything was put on hold. I delivered my first son, Abdul Rahman, in July of 2001. At twenty-four, a month after giving birth, I registered my business name, "Build Self Group," as a domain name and started searching for a web design company to create my web site.

Since taking my first steps in business, I have learned from my mistakes, lost money to vendors who over-promised and under-delivered, and gained a second Master's degree in Management and in Coaching and Mentoring and a third in Education and Training. I wanted to use my academic grounding in a useful way, because many entrepreneurs – like Richard Branson and Bill Gates – have no formal education or have not completed their higher education. I also started focusing my business on women in the community and women entrepreneurs. I registered my business profile on ecademy.com and linkedin.com, and started a networking and coaching group on collectivex.com, taking my business online and increasing the membership as I network with inspiring women professionals and businessmen. I'm starting a collaboration movement that I call a business revolution!

I'm enjoying every minute of the experience. I don't feel like I'm working because my business is my passion; it fulfills my life purpose. It has been a long journey from my humble beginnings, and I look forward to continuing to build my business from the ground up. My customers and members are the driving force for my business: without them I have no business. They make me push my boundaries further and venture into uncharted waters with courage, clear vision, and a united purpose.

How have you created your life on your terms?

I had to be strong in character, and in faith. I had to believe in myself, and believe that people are truly good. As Dr. Muhammad Yunis (the creator of the "microcredit" concept, and founder of the Grameen Bank in Bangledesh, which provides loans to entrepreneurs too poor to start their businesses) once said: "We are all entrepreneurs, just some realize it and others don't."

What have you learned from mentors and role models in your life?

I have been mentored over the years by many people, but mainly by my friend Brenda Childs Berry; Irum Khan Lodhi, Lawyer and Entrepreneur; Fowzia al Kessiri; and my volunteer manager Steve Tarrant from the West Howe Network. These people had unquestioning faith in me and always believed that I had something more to contribute to society. I thank them all for their support, and I am still in contact with and close to all of them today, because they are friends for life.

I first received my inspiration from my father. He inspired me to be the best, to serve the local community, to challenge the status quo, to live a dignified life, and to be a leader. I also have been inspired by various community and business leaders who have made a difference at a local, community, or international level – namely, Lady Diana, Princess of Wales; Margaret Thatcher; Mother Theresa; Queen Rania of Jordan; Oprah Winfrey; and news presenter Zainab Badawi.

Please share one tip for living a full life:

As Winston Churchill once said in a speech delivered to university graduates: "Never give up, never give up, never give up!"

What would you like your legacy to be?

That I achieved as much as I could in the little time I had on this earth, enabling and empowering women from the international community to build their lives and businesses around everlasting principles: sharing, caring, leading, creating, building, living free and independently, and loving the self.

Ilham's Message:

The business revolution starts with empowered, educated women who support and inspire each other.

FELICIA J. SLATTERY

*"The way we communicate with others and with ourselves
ultimately determines the quality of our lives."*
- Tony Robbins

Felicia is a communication consultant, speaker, and coach specializing in training busy professionals to succeed by communicating effectively. After she nearly lost her life giving birth to her daughter, Felicia felt she had learned a great lesson, and decided that she wanted to reach and inspire people through teaching.

For Felicia, creating life on her own terms meant working for herself, and most importantly, setting her own schedule. She wanted to be able to be a parent during the day, and do her own thing at night. She believes that planning within your passion, acting rather than reacting, is the best way to achieve success.

What inspired you to become an entrepreneur?

I think I've been an entrepreneur my entire life. I was the kid with the lemonade stand, and I sold tickets to backyard productions of plays the neighborhood kids and I wrote ourselves! In high school I took on a leadership role in a Junior Achievement program where we started a business as part of a class, developed a product, and sold it for a substantial profit.

In my twenties, I began a direct sales business, and that's when I learned how much I enjoyed doing real work on my own terms. My current business, Communication Transformation, was founded in early 2006, when, after nearly losing my life in childbirth, I realized I wanted to be home with my children while still contributing both to my family's bottom line and to society. My "why" is my family, and living my life on my own terms means dedicating time to them.

How have you created your life on your terms?

Whenever I have made a decision to pursue a major goal, I have gone after it and achieved it. Nothing stops me from achieving what I want, because I know that with enough work and time, anyone can accomplish whatever they set their mind to. Things don't always come easily, but persistence always pays off!

One of the biggest mistakes I see people make is living in "reaction" mode. Instead of looking at their lives, their skills, and their dreams, and using that information to take charge of their own destinies, they allow people and situations to guide what they experience. A crucial element in creating a life on your terms is to decide what your terms are. That takes some introspection, reflection, and personal development to fully realize – but when you do, look out world! Being clear on what you want is the first step toward having it in your life.

What have you learned from mentors and role models in your life?

I've learned from many different teachers in many different situations. I tend to learn moment by moment. However, beyond being aware of the learning opportunities all around me on a daily basis, I have worked with several "official" mentors in my life. Those people have helped me shape who I am today. I couldn't point to just one lesson; there have been so many. I think it's imperative that everyone find a mentor they can work with, ask questions of, and lean on for support as they find their way toward success.

Please share one tip for living a full life:

Living a full life means being fully present, and fully experiencing the little moments that make up an entire lifetime. Most people plan for the big or major moments – like birthdays, weddings, anniversaries, holidays and events – but many of those come just once a year, or even once in a lifetime. The key to living a full life is to never underestimate the power of the tiniest moments: the smell of your baby after a bath, the giggles of little girls playing happily, rolling down the windows and cranking the car radio while you sing your favorite song at the top of your lungs, the taste of a favorite meal, the joy in a sunrise or sunset, or getting lost in the hug of a good friend. Stop rushing around, slow down, notice the world around you, and be grateful for the smallest gifts.

You'll hear people say, "Do what you're passionate about; do what you love," and I can't agree more – but you need to do it on your own terms by creating your own actions, as opposed to reacting to what other people say or do. Planning within your passion, acting rather than reacting, is the best way to achieve your success.

What would you like your legacy to be?

My legacy will be what I teach my two young daughters. As I watch them grow, I hope that they will learn to experience the small moments in life; that they won't constantly be looking forward, but rather that they'll be looking at where they are now and be grateful for all they have. I would like to teach them they can do anything they set their minds to, just as my mother taught me – and I want them to believe it and prove it just like I did!

In terms of the bigger picture, I want something similar: I want people everywhere to realize that your dreams don't have to wait until someday or later. You can start now. Also, I firmly believe we all have a message to share with the world. Understanding and learning effective communication skills will help people everywhere get their message to those who need it most, while enhancing their most important professional and personal relationships.

Felicia's Message:

Plan within your passion and do it on your own terms. Share what you've learned with the world.

CHAPTER 5

Unconventional Wisdom

"The price of anything is the amount of life you exchange for it."
- Henry David Thoreau

Conventional wisdom tells us that in order to succeed you have to get a good job, work your ass off, climb the corporate ladder rung by rung, and start living when you retire.

I'll tell you right now: that's ridiculous.

The current world economic state is shaking things up, opening the floodgates of entrepreneurial opportunity and making the old standards obsolete. There is no more "business as usual." We can no longer count on big companies to support us just because we put the time in – as many who have been laid off or downsized can attest. (However, as we explored in the last chapter, the discomfort of being laid off can easily become an opportunity to explore new frontiers.)

It's no surprise that the business world has become information- and service-based. The twenty-first century brought with it a new way of thinking, behaving, and winning in business. A new breed of entrepreneurs – including virtual coaches, virtual assistants, freelance writers, graphic designers, videographers, internet marketers, bloggers, and web designers – are making things happen. Business partnerships based on super-charged collaborative efforts are cropping up all over the place. Successful small business owners are bartering their way to success by surrounding themselves with brilliant people willing to exchange their talents for services instead of cash. Profitable relationships are created via Twitter, Facebook, Linkedin and other social networks – in fact, I met the majority of the people I interviewed for this book through social media. There's a whole new virtual, viral world right at our fingertips, and all we have to do is plug in.

Unconventional wisdom teaches us to get clear about what we want right now, at this stage of the game, and make it happen quickly. According to an economic study aired on National Public Radio (NPR) in the summer of 2009, the most lucrative career choices for future generations will include visual arts, graphic design, photography, and videography – in other words, careers which support the enormous appetite of the virtual world. Bloggers like Leo Babauta of Zen Habits and Brian Clark of Copy Blogger are swimming right alongside mainstream journalists, making a healthy living on their content and attracting droves of subscribers.

To proponents of this new, unconventional wisdom, the idea of slaving away for a soulless corporation is no longer tolerable. These people have recognized that it's not okay for managers to treat employees poorly, no matter how sweet the benefits package; for them, the thought of "sticking it out" holds about as much appeal as a life sentence in a state prison. Meanwhile, while the entrepreneurial movement gains steam, corporate revolutionaries gather in the wings, ready to run with the message "Change or Die!" With entrepreneurship a viable option for just about anyone willing to make the leap, fear is no longer enough to keep employees toeing the line.

When I was still riding the corporate train, I witnessed decision-makers unwilling to change what they saw as a perfectly good paradigm. "Why change the way we roll," they asked, "if the cows are still producing milk and the calves are getting fat?" There was no room for negotiation or even conversation, and no chance for real issues to come to light. Certainly there was no room for a win-win scenario.

Alas, the days of decision-makers golfing all summer long while the cash magically rolls in are finished for the foreseeable future. Because when upper management micro-manages, alienates, and eventually lays off middle management, who will run the business while they are out on the links?

Once upon a time, ship captains would cast traitors and thieves overboard with concrete shoes on their feet. Old-school corporations are sinking just as quickly – only this time, the suspects are dipping their own feet into the cement. How can employment freezes, pay cuts, and layoffs of tenured employees take place on the same day that the executives' pimped-out SUVs arrive from the dealership? Do they really think their employees don't notice?

For years I swam with the rest of the fishes, followed most of the rules, and actually believed the story of "The Way of the Professional Woman." Today I see that I was a visionary trapped in an ancient paradigm. The regime I worked for had no interest in anything but fear-based power and the bottom line. What this group and so many like it fail to realize is that their company is a living and breathing organism, not an impenetrable fortress. Now, years after my departure, the company in which I invested so much time has lost loads of revenue and many brilliant employees. The curious thing is, the current leadership couldn't care less. They're too busy making excuses to notice that their fortress is crumbling around them.

I fancy myself an unconventional woman. It's fun to be different. Instead of going with the flow, now I'm swimming against the tide of conventional thinking in order to fully embrace my life and what I want from it. Even better, I know that what I do might inspire someone else to be authentic, and to create a life which leads them to a place they want to show up to. After all, that's what creating life on your terms is all about!

It has been my observation that healthy personal development, as well as success in business, absolutely depends on aligning your business goals with your lifestyle choices and core values.

Whether or not your entrepreneurial vision includes employees, it can be really helpful to create a core values statement. Not only will it serve as a reminder of why you're doing what you do, it can help you find customers whose values are aligned with your ideals. Many people I know would rather spend more to buy organic food grown by local farmers, or get a cup of coffee from a place where the employees are happy and personable. But if those vendors didn't advertise their core values (fair trade, organic, employee-centric, etc.) many of their customers would never have found them. It all comes down to the Law of Attraction: what you put out there comes back to you!

Speaking of core values...

Zappos is a hugely successful online business that sells shoes, handbags, sunglasses and clothing with free shipping on all merchandise both ways.

Tony Hsieh, CEO of Zappos and participant in this project, published the following statement on the Zappos web site:

> As we grow as a company, it has become more and more important to explicitly define the Zappos core values from which we develop our culture, our brand, and our business strategies. These are the ten core values that we live by:
>
> 1. Deliver WOW Through Service
>
> 2. Embrace and Drive Change
>
> 3. Create Fun and A Little Weirdness
>
> 4. Be Adventurous, Creative, and Open-Minded
>
> 5. Pursue Growth and Learning
>
> 6. Build Open and Honest Relationships with Communication
>
> 7. Build a Positive Team and Family Spirit
>
> 8. Do More With Less
>
> 9. Be Passionate and Determined
>
> 10. Be Humble

What's not to love about a company that supports a little weirdness!

Core values are more meaningful and transparent than conventional corporate mission statements. No wonder Zappos is considered one of the top 100 companies to work for according to *Inc. Magazine.* Amazon.com was so impressed they bought Zappos in 2009 for more than $900,000.

Flying in the face of convention, Tim Ferriss urges us to join the "New Rich" by leaving the conventional rat race in his *New York Times* bestseller The *4-Hour Work Week*. I highly recommend Tim's book to help you wrap your brain around an interesting, creative and potentially lucrative way of being in the new paradigm of business. You can also check out my favorite marketer, Seth Godin, author of *Linchpin, The Purple Cow, Tribes, Meatball Sundae* and many other titles. By reminding us there are not enough leaders in the world, Godin is urging us to step up and lead a tribe of our own in this new creative and independent business landscape.

At this moment, everything is up for review and change. You owe it to yourself to embrace the opportunities of a brave new world which values integrity, collaboration, and core values.

Read on to meet a brilliant group of highly unconventional and extremely creative entrepreneurs.

MATT LAMPHERE

"To hell with circumstances: I create opportunities."

- Bruce Lee

All of his life, Matt Lamphere felt he was destined to go beyond the status quo. The corporate culture of rules and regulations felt unsavory to him. Eventually, he found himself in a position where he could continue working for others or become the architect of his own life. Now, he has a deep love for his work – he'd even do it for free, if he didn't have to pay bills!

By directing his energies toward abundance, and being thankful for what he has instead of worrying about what he lacks, he attracts what he is designed for, and has been extremely successful in his new endeavors.

What inspired you to become an entrepreneur?

It chose me, really. Ever since I was a child, I felt that I was built for more than just maintaining the status quo. That, and I never could play well under other people's rules and regulations. I find the environment of most corporate cultures to be unsavory. I have always been more mission-driven, preferring to work project to project, as opposed to adhering to a conventional 9-to-5 business model.

For reasons beyond my grasp, I have a deep love for my work. I have even tried leaving my industry, and nothing else fits quite right. I would do this work for free, if not for those pesky bills that need attending to. The work fulfills me, and after spending my early years working for others, I found myself in a position where I had to either continue seeking employment, or sail my own pirate ship.

It was not until around twelve years into my career that I finally, quietly, understood what I was here on this earth to do. There is something deeply peaceful about attaining the knowledge of one's own purpose. It was like, "Finally! I can get to work and stop going through the motions!" An opportunity presented itself, and I left the broadcast industry permanently.

Understand, I left a job as a department head with a decent salary, an all-expenses-paid company vehicle, an expense account, ample vacation pay, 401k, insurance, etc. I walked away from it all, took an enormous pay cut and jumped without a safety net.

That opportunity I left my comfortable job for ... It didn't work.

So, I took a job at a bar as a short order cook and occasional bartender-in-training. This, as it turns out, was a blast, and it kept me alive while I launched my own production company. There were days when I had just enough gas in my car to make it to work; if not for the tips I earned I would not have made it home that night. I learned many valuable lessons from that experience.

Within two years, my new business took off, and my very first year out I doubled the income that I was earning at the old TV station gig. The point of this story has nothing to do with the money: I could care less about that. As long as I have ample cash flow to operate my life, I'm happy. The point is that by directing my energies toward abundance and being ever thankful for simple existence and the beauty of life, I know I attract what I am designed for.

I'm an entrepreneur simply because I must do what I do. I don't have a choice in the matter. It's not a perfect life. It is, however, my life, and I love it, perfectly.

How have you created your life on your terms?

On my twenty-fifth birthday, I made the very conscious choice to Be Happy. It occurred to me that being happy was something that required effort, and the only way to achieve this much-desired state of being was to alter my thought patterns and effectively change my perception of the world around me – to release control and accept the fact that the only thing that I can truly affect is my world-view and how I handle my day-to-day living. This made a profound shift in my life.

I was in an interesting place. Most days I vacillated between wanting to be a Samurai, or a ditch digger – anything but what I was. I tried wearing several different costumes. I immersed myself in the study of philosophy, theology, and the martial arts. Through that turbulent exercise I came to understand, with perfect clarity, that you, me, us...We personally craft our existence, completely and without question, each and every one of us. I am the architect of my life.

I chose to take responsibility for all of my actions, good and bad. I understood that a happy, meaningful life wasn't anything that I was owed, or that I deserved by some universal definition of entitlement. I also did not buy into the dogma that if you follow the formulaic American Dream; go to school, get married, make babies, get in more debt that you can handle, retire, and die... Presto, you'll have the perfect life, white picket fence and all. That's garbage. Complete, utter garbage. Not to say that does not work for some, but certainly it does not work for me.

My happiness is not defined by how I measure up to others, or where I am on the continuum of that traditional scale. I have all the power and raw material to build my world exactly the way that I want it. When I fail, it is due to my action, and when I succeed, I am blessed. To me the greatest part about having this gift of life is that we get to build it the way we want it.

I am apocalyptically imperfect on a cosmic scale at times, and I flounder a lot, but I never give up. I believe, completely and without any indecision, that I will achieve absolutely everything that I set out to do, sooner or later. Along with that, I reserve the right to change my mind at a moment's notice.

I trust my intuition. It has never let me down. My soul has things to say, if listened to. Whether it's divine connection with the

Source or just really great poker instincts, I don't care. I tap into it, and listen to what it says.

What have you learned from mentors and role models in your life?

I never had anyone take me under their wing, so to speak. But, there are a handful of people who I deeply admire, and I have learned different things from each of them. They are all specialists in their respective vocations, and great people. They come from different walks of life: martial arts instructors, yoga instructors, other entrepreneurs, that guy at the TV station who taught me how to edit when I was eighteen, my high school TV production teacher, cinematographers, tradesmen, and family...The list goes on. All of my role models have inspired me with their innovation, curiosity, passion, and drive, and by being true to their essence.

Please share one tip for living a full life:

Listen to your heart, always. Follow your intuition and strive for complete awareness. Seek the complete moment. The Japanese have a word, Zanshin, which means "alertness." They have another, Mushin, which means, roughly, "No Mind." To perform with the complete presence of all your senses, truly savoring and experiencing the fullness of each moment of your existence – whether you are doing your laundry, riding a motorcycle, snapping a photograph, or just simply being – seek the Mushin of the moment. A life focused on this endeavor is an amazing state of being to live in, in my opinion.

What would you like your legacy to be?

On my tombstone: Matt Lamphere, he saved the world...a lot! Seriously, though, before I slip the mortal coil, I will create something visual that affects people – that makes them think, that has an impact on a profound level. What would that be? I have no idea...yet.

That, and I would like to be regarded as a guy who noticed beauty, and really liked the movie *Ghostbusters*.

Matt's Message:

Don't fall into the trap of living your life in a way that suits others. Operate from a place of abundance and happiness, and you will always have the life you want and deserve.

Leo Babauta

"Smile, breathe, and go slowly."

- Thich Nhat Hanh

In 2007, Leo Babauta found his true calling, and quit his job to pursue his passion as a personal development blogger. He is inspired by others' success stories, and is grateful to know he is not alone in his quest for happiness.

One of the first steps Leo took on his path was creating a list of the things that were most important to him. When he found that his life did not reflect those things, he changed his focus, and started building his life around what really mattered: family, writing, reading, and running. Leo cleared his life of clutter by saying "no" to things that interfered with his core values. This freed him up to pursue the things he loves most with passion and determination.

What inspired you to become an entrepreneur?

All my life, I worked for others as a journalist, legislative analyst, and speech writer, until I discovered my true passion: blogging. In 2007, I found my calling, and decided that I wanted to quit my day job so that I could be free to pursue this passion. I dedicated an entire year to making the transition from employee to entrepreneur.

It wasn't easy, and I had to be really focused, but since I loved what I was doing it was an exciting journey. When I quit my day job in January 2008, I was elated and ecstatic. I've never loved anything more than I've loved working for myself, and I hope never to be anything other than an entrepreneur.

What inspires me most is seeing the positive changes I've helped others accomplish. When you've contributed to a life change, it is gratifying, and makes you want to continue to do good. I'm inspired as well by the successes of others – the people who prove to me daily that miracles are possible, and that I'm not alone in my quest for happiness.

How have you created your life on your terms?

Three years ago, I made a list of the things that are most important to me: spending time with my family, writing, reading and running. My life didn't reflect these things at that time, but slowly I've built my life around these four essential things. It took a lot of focus to clear my life of clutter so that I'd have room for the things I love, and to say no to everything that tried to take my time away from these things. Today I'm happy to say that my life is the life I've always dreamed of, and is based around the things I love most.

I'm also happy to say that I'm my own boss for the first time ever. I am answerable only to my own dreams and values, which is an incredibly liberating thing.

What have you learned from mentors and role models in your life?

I didn't have a mentor in the traditional sense – someone who took me under his or her wing and guided me along the way – but I've had many people who have inspired me in what they're doing: Gina Trapani and Adam Pash of Lifehacker; J.D. Roth of Get Rich Slowly; Darren Rowse of Problogger; Brian Clark of Copyblogger; Stephen Covey; and many other bloggers, writers, and authors. Some have even offered their help and advice at different points along the way. I'm grateful to all of them, even if I can't name them all.

Please share one tip for living a full life:

Be passionate about whatever you do – whether it's your work, spending time with loved ones, getting fit and healthy, taking up a hobby, creating, or starting a new business. If you haven't found something to be passionate about, start looking now, and don't stop until you find it. Then, don't be afraid to pursue it with all the passion you have!

What would you like your legacy to be?

My grandfather died at the age of eighty-one. He lived a full life, had a great career, and traveled the world. He left behind a large and loving family, and was mourned by hundreds of friends. I would like to leave this earth with a life and friends and family behind me like that. I'd like to say that I loved and was loved, and that I helped others and learned from them.

Leo's Message:

Identify how you want to live your life and make small changes toward those goals. Take stock of your values and ask yourself if you're living in a way that honors them. When you find your calling, pursue it with passion and purpose.

GABE ZICHERMANN

"If five people tell you you're drunk, lie down."
- Elias Gergely

Gabe Zichermann was ten years old when he began selling shoes and purses alongside his mother at weekend markets, and the entrepreneurial spirit has been with him ever since. His humble beginnings gave Gabe an interesting perspective on business.

After a six-year manic ride through technology madness, Gabe sold his first company for $35 million and learned a big lesson about the importance of aligning yourself with the right people. His experience convinced him that no matter what happens, you can always figure out a way to make the best of a situation.

What inspired you to become an entrepreneur?

My parents were defectors from communist countries. In the late 1960s, they came to Toronto, Canada, where I grew up. My dad has a tremendously positive attitude toward work. Before he retired a few years ago, he worked for an airline in Canada, and went to work every single day with a smile on his face. He's a morning person too, so watching him get up in the morning was pretty amazing.

On the flip side, my mom was always an entrepreneur: she had no desire to work for someone else. All throughout my childhood she ran small businesses. One of her friends ran an import/export company, and so my mom started selling fancy imported shoes from Europe at the markets that took place around Toronto on the weekends. When I was nine or so, I started going with her. We'd pack up the van at 4:00 a.m. and drive to the outlying towns where they had the markets. My mom was arguably the best salesperson I've ever met – shockingly good. I was about ten when I started actively selling, and I learned a lot of interesting lessons from her. When I was sixteen, we launched one of my first entrepreneurial ventures: a family printing business. The company did really well for the first year. Then, we raised a bit of outside money and we collapsed – a spectacular failure in the recession of the early 1990s. I had to lay off twenty people at the age of seventeen. It was an early lesson.

The first company I helped start as an adult was a technology company called Tri Media. I was an early starter (I finished grad school at twenty-one), and we launched the company in 1999, at the height of the boom.

Just a couple years after starting the company, we entered that really brutal first tech recession. We went from raising money and having lots of cash and perks to once again laying off a whole bunch of people, drawing the company down to its very core, and literally running out of money. It was a dramatic reversal of fortune in a short amount of time, a scenario which was all too familiar to me. But this time, the power to persevere was there. Our core team was focused on success, and we all agreed that it was worthwhile to continue to roll the dice. We'd gotten into this because we were risk-positive people, we decided, so why give up now?

We weathered that storm, and a couple of years later, after a lot of action, our market turned around. After we'd been in business for six years, people started making offers on our company, and we sold Tri Media in 2005 for $35 million.

While $35 million wasn't the number I had hoped for when we went into business, in my years with Tri Media I learned Big Life Lesson #3: alignment between people is the most important thing in the world. (In case you're wondering, Timing is Lesson #2, and Happiness is Lesson #1.)

I remember one really important lesson from my mom – my foundation story. When I was in my teens, someone came into our shop. I was trying to sell him something and he was being pretty rude to me. My mom was in the back, but when she overheard the conversation she came out and said, "I think you should leave the store." The man said, "Are you being serious? I can't believe you're doing this to me!" She repeated herself. It wasn't an escalation, she just asked him to leave.

After the person left, I said, "I was trying to make a sale! I could have sold to that guy!" She said, "Honey, don't forget: it's your store." She wasn't trying to protect me; she was trying to teach me a lesson.

How have you created your life on your terms?

It's pretty tough for a bright young person who's not a math genius to become an entrepreneur, especially when you come from a humble background.

A lot of entrepreneurs are wealthy. I know this shatters an entrepreneurship myth, but the reality is that most guys and girls who start companies have money already. That was not the case for my working-class family. Nonetheless, they put whatever money they could into my business.

It would be really easy for me to take a big job at some big company, draw a salary, and travel around the world as a pundit (which is a part-time thing that I do). In order not to do this, I've had to forego the basic comfort that every immigrant child grows up learning about. I know it sounds like a small challenge, but when my parents hear what kind of money I leave on the table from a job standpoint, it's tough for them to understand. They don't get why I won't take that job that pays me a lot of money – the job that every immigrant hopes their child will get. I have lots of peers that have that kind of lifestyle, but I created life on my terms by believing in myself and following my instincts, and I'm not going to stop now.

What have you learned from mentors and role models in your life?

A number of people have been extraordinarily kind and generous with me along the way. I try to pay it forward every opportunity I get. These extraordinary folks include a graduate school professor, Barry Render, who offered an unbelievable amount of support; and Karen Kaplowitz, who has been instrumental in offering her guidance these last few years.

Probably one of the most interesting moments of mentorship didn't really feel like mentorship at all (at the time). During grad school, I was interning at an early EMR (Electronic Medical Records) company called Visteon. Things were going very well, and I felt confident that I would get a full-time position after school. In the February of my final year, the company's president invited me to lunch. Over lunch, he told me that he, my boss, and the company's CEO had decided that I should leave Visteon once school was over. In their opinion, I could not grow to my full potential there, and needed to move to the Bay Area to fulfill my dream of tech entrepreneurship.

I was devastated. Not only did I love the job and the people, but I hadn't spent any energy looking for post-school work, since I thought my future at Visteon was all but guaranteed. I felt as though I was being fired, and very much like a failure, despite their protestations to the contrary. Of course, I eventually got over myself and took a position at the (then burgeoning) Cisco Systems in San Jose and began my career. In retrospect, they did one of the nicest things for me that anyone has ever done.

Please share one tip for living a full life:

My grandfather, who was not a Mr. Wisecrack kind of guy, once said: "If five people tell you you're drunk, lie down." I think it's important to remember that when you're a motivated, creatively driven person, you're often way out ahead of yourself, even if you don't realize it. Throughout my late teens and early twenties, people would say, "You've done so much for someone your age!" I'd respond by saying that their observation didn't even compute. I'd never been in someone else's experience, so to me the observation didn't make sense. Now I look back, and realize that yes, I was definitely ahead of myself. I was doing some interesting things and didn't realize how far I had gone. It's important to listen to the people around you, not necessarily to change what you're going to do, but to hear a conceptualization of what they have to tell you.

What would you like your legacy to be?

When you're staring down the mouth of a potential really big defeat – like when you realize that the market isn't great right now, and there's a very real possibility your business may fail – when you start to turn that over in your mind, you start to get philosophical. Lately, I've been thinking a lot about that "drive," and I think we're all driven to create a legacy. Some people have kids, or leave an endowment. I'm trying to think of it more in terms of what would be true to me.

In all honesty, I feel like I need to change the way people do stuff. I've already done that in a small way: twice in my career, I've done something that has fundamentally changed a behavior. Now, I want to make a lasting and permanent change in how the world works.

Gabe's Message:

Following your passion is never about money. Happiness, timing and relationships are the most important things in the world. Do all you can to leave a lasting impression on the people with whom you communicate and interact.

TOM CLYNES

"The secret to getting ahead is getting started."

- Mark Twain

Tom Clynes created a life on his own terms because he couldn't do it any other way. He tried working in offices, but didn't enjoy having to be in the office at the same time every day, and answer for his whereabouts. He felt accountability should be based on output.

Now, Tom spends a lot of time traveling to rural environments in Asia, Australia, the South Pacific, Africa, and New Zealand. He enjoys reporting in places that are off the beaten path, and tells stories about environmental issues, conservation, adventure travel, and science. Bombing around in old trucks and light airplanes brings him great joy, as does writing extraordinary stories about his experiences.

Tom believes his willingness to make friends with vulnerability, uncertainty, and risk has been the key to success in his life and business.

What inspired you to become an entrepreneur?

I grew up in Michigan. Saginaw, mostly. I was always convinced that there was something a little bit more interesting 'out there', so when I got a bug to travel, I went to the East Coast. Then, I and came back, did college, started writing, and went off to travel again after I graduated from the university. I moved to England, then to Berlin, then kept on going through Europe, South America, Asia, Australia, and the South Pacific.

At some point, I started trying to reconcile the travel thing with the writing thing. I was very interested in both, but I didn't know how to make it happen. I had some luck with commercial writing, things like advertising copy and speeches for executives. I would go off for several months and travel around, then come back and get some freelance work. It was quite lucrative working for the automotive companies and others, but after a while I thought, "Okay, I'm not going to change the world by selling more Volvos or oil filters." I started looking at ways to bring the travel and the writing together.

I had an idea for a book project called "Wild Planet." It was about festivals, celebrations, events, and tribal gatherings all over the world. I really loved going to festivals when traveling. I thought, "That's really the best time to drop in on the locals: when they're on a binge." You see a place as it is when people let their hair down, and there's not so much a transactional approach to visitors; it can be more of a friendship. Places are more open, more vibrant and alive when people are partying. I thought I'd do a guide to the world's extraordinary events, and that book became *Wild Planet: 1001 Extraordinary Events for Inspired Travel.* It came out in 1995.

I did another book in 1996 about music festivals, but I was really looking to write less about travel and more about environmental issues, public health, and adventure. So I started working my way into the magazine publishing world. I didn't get far at first; I didn't understand how the business worked, and I didn't understand how you get in. Turns out, it's extremely difficult to get in. I kind of struggled my way in the side door. I started doing minor things for minor publications, getting hardly any money and even less respect.

Eventually, I reported a story in Australia about a big-rig driver who delivers fuel to a very remote northern part of the Outback — very tropical, muddy and dusty at times. He was always breaking down and sometimes got attacked by crocodiles and snakes. I rode with him for six days. That story was published in the inaugural edition of *National Geographic Adventure* in 1999. It was titled, "The World's Toughest Trucker". I guess you could call that one of my big breaks.

I started writing regularly for *National Geographic Adventure* and decided I would give every story my all and make it the very best it could be. I probably put way too much time into things, but I was convinced this was the way to do it. I wanted everybody to be very happy with every story; I wanted people to talk about my stories. I wanted my stories to be influential and I wanted my stories in some way to change the world. I started writing a lot about conservation, especially in Africa. I started writing about very unusual schemes for raising eco-mercenary militias to protect elephants and drive poachers out of the Central African Republic. I wrote about genocide in Rwanda and the gorillas. I was in Asia a lot; also Australia and elsewhere in the South Pacific.

How have you created your life on your terms?

I'm doing it out of necessity, essentially, because I couldn't do it any other way. I tried working in offices for a while. I didn't enjoy being accountable for being there at certain times of the day. I thought accountability should be based on the quality and quantity of output. I don't like working under bad fluorescent lighting and all the rules and politics. I just wasn't really cut out for that environment. I can be a team player, but maybe not every single work day of the year. I needed to build something for myself that would be more flexible. I think I probably work harder than I would if I had just about any corporate job. The old joke is, "I'm self-employed, which means I can work any fourteen hours of the day I want to!" I love the freedom, I love the independence, I'm so driven by curiosity that I need to put myself in situations where I can explore things. It just feels necessary.

I think one of the keys to making this happen was that, when I was building my globe-trotting career, I was single, with no kids. I waited a long time to have kids; I waited until my career was established, which was a good and bad thing because my particular career is not all that compatible with the domestic side of life. Had I had children earlier, I'm quite sure I never would have gotten to have this kind of career.

Material comfort isn't all that important to me. I actually like to get my hands dirty. I like having my own office, setting up my own space. I have allowed myself to be vulnerable. Really, that's what travel is all about, whether it's vulnerability in a real sense (physical security) or vulnerability in terms of feeling insecure because you don't understand the language or the culture and don't know anybody. Being willing to make friends with vulnerability, uncertainty and risk has been the key for this kind of career.

What have you learned from mentors and role models in your life?

I've interviewed and observed some of the world's most accomplished explorers, conservationists, doctors, virus hunters, diplomats, and mountain climbers. So when it comes to accomplishment, I've been very fortunate: I have been able to learn from the masters, from people who have turned once-ordinary lives into extraordinary, world-changing adventures. What sets them apart is tenacity and risk-taking. They've been tenacious in developing the skills and expertise to be world-class at whatever they do. And they've been willing to continue to take risks, to keep reaching.

Please share one tip for living a full life:

Being willing to take risks is the main thing. Don't weigh yourself down with material things to the point that you are no longer able to walk away from those things. The average American could sell his or her car and travel around the world for two years. Travel doesn't need to be expensive: in fact, that's one of the great fallacies of travel. For me, travel is still mostly about independence and satisfying curiosity. I need to find out, for myself, what's going on out there.

What would you like your legacy to be?

Professionally, I want to create extraordinary stories. I want to keep perfecting my craft to the extent that when people read my stories, they are touched by my stories; they feel moved to do something.

Then there's my personal legacy, which involves my children. I want my children to grow up confident, compassionate and happy.

Tom's Message:

Make friends with vulnerability. Take risks and allow creativity to blossom in the places you least expect.

CHAPTER 6

Trusting in the Universe

"Thoughts Become Things... Choose the Good Ones!™*"*
- Mike Dooley

We are involved in one of the most fascinating times in human history. Malnourished from years of fear-based conditioning, abuse of power and "it's all about the bottom line" greed, our steadfast rules and ideals have come undone, paving the way for radical change. Intuitive, creative and compassionate creatures, rather than being shunted aside (or worse, persecuted), will instead fare quite well for the foreseeable future. The new world is shedding her collective ego, allowing the laws of the universe to permeate every molecule of her being.

More than ever before, we're challenging corporations, and our questions are turning political regimes upside down. We're leaving organized religion in droves to connect with our spirituality on our own terms. New world entrepreneurs are choosing a spiritual path of independence, loving kindness, morality, and integrity by embracing their unique calling and trusting in community.

Movies like *The Secret*, which teaches the Law of Attraction, are being embraced by the mainstream. *What the Bleep Do We Know!?*, once labeled a cult classic, is now a must-see documentary for unconventional thinkers. The popularity of Dr. Wayne Dyer's book, *Change Your Thoughts – Change Your Life*, is another example of how much our paradigms are shifting. Dr. Dyer researched and meditated on Lao-Tzu's ancient *Tao Te Ching*, or "Way of Life," and his book is the result. The verses written by Lao-Tzu, a highly spiritual man who lived five hundred years before Christ, are as appropriate for spiritual seekers today as they were in Lao-Tzu's time.

Esoteric teachings, once labeled as "woo-woo" or "bizarre hippie notions," have been cracked open wide like fresh coconuts, and are being devoured by millions of people who are ready to trust in the Universe and take their faith, and their fate, into their own hands.

Trust in the benevolence of the Universe, and belief in the power of setting an intention, attracted brilliant people like Tony Hsieh, Nic Askew, Alicia Castillo Holley, and Arlene Battishill to this project. Rather than hoarding their secrets for entrepreneurial freedom, each individual was excited by the thought that their experience could make a difference to someone else.

> In order to grow your business, ask yourself these questions:
>
> - Who do you know?
> - How can you help them?
> - Who do you trust?
> - What are they great at?
> - How can they participate in growing your business?
> - Which of your talents can you share with them?

Advisory boards are now made of talented friends and business associates, rather than hired "experts." No longer afraid to share our dreams and passions, we are able to let go of corporate red tape and fear-based attachment to old ideas. Brilliant projects come together every day, and a collective smile is shared by all involved. Why? Because we've invited trusted, talented people to join us on our mission, and in return, we will help them create their own dreams. It's teamwork redefined!

Highly talented people enjoy being of service to each other without sending an invoice for sharing their time and expertise. Even tiny start-ups can grow into healthy businesses without big backing and venture capital if they trade their services mindfully and with gratitude; instead of investing dollars, they invest their expertise. When service to one another is our highest priority, there's nothing we can't do.

An international tax-accountant-turned-entrepreneur, Mike Dooley, is one of the teachers for the best-selling book and DVD *The Secret*. Mike runs TUT's Adventurers Club. He also speaks to thousands internationally about life, dreams, and happiness. Dooley claims that walking away from the corporate world and a large salary to start over at zero is his greatest achievement. Mike is a role model for anybody toying with the idea of leaving the corporate world, and a poster boy for trust in the Universe.

The process of uncovering your calling and learning to trust in yourself, your passion, and the Universe is like riding a wave of pure, unbridled joy. When the wave crests, you're suddenly on top of the world – but you might also find a wash of peacefulness tugging at the corner of your lips, the promise of a smile.

Everything you dream of can become your reality. But first, you have to believe in your dreams, and that means trusting not only yourself, but something greater than yourself. While I was living this process, I created an "Inbox to Universe" filled with statements like, "I am in the process of becoming a highly successful and inspirational coach," "I am a best-selling coauthor," "I am a certified yoga instructor, and enjoy teaching yoga play-shops across the country," "I have enough money to live comfortably and give back to my community," "I attract creative entrepreneurs and powerful women in career transition to my coaching business," and, "I am healthy

> Do you agree that you become what you think about?
>
> • Are your most common thoughts about your dreams and aspirations positive or negative?
>
> • According to the Law of Attraction, thinking, "I need…" creates more need, but thinking, "I am in the process of…" or "I have…" draws those things to you. How can you restructure your daily mantras (or "inbox messages") to resonate more powerfully in the Universe?

and happy." I add new statements to the inbox as often as I wish, and at the end of each month I look at the messages to make sure they still resonate with me. My inbox has become a direct line of connection to my higher power, and a worthy method of support. How do I know it works? In three short years, each of the aforementioned dreams has materialized!

If you really want to get things moving, I recommend the book *The Law of Attraction* by Michael Losier, a practical guide to putting the Universal laws into action. Unlike many books of its kind, *The Law of Attraction* is written totally in layman's terms, and even includes some workbook features and exercises to get you started.

The next batch of interviews features entrepreneurs who live in abundance, trust in the Universe, and practice the Law of Attraction.

AKEMI GAINES

"Others have seen what is, and asked 'Why?'
I have seen what could be and asked, 'Why not?'"

- Picasso

Akemi Gaines had a comfortable life in Japan, but internally, she felt suffocated. She knew she had a purpose in life beyond just living comfortably, and was ready to dump the comfort for the sake of her own personal growth.

Akemi took a leap of faith because she believed she could help people in a unique way. Today, she has a successful practice called Akashic Record Reading, through which she helps those who are serious about their spiritual growth. She also writes the Real Life Spirituality Blog, which is dedicated to inspiring people to create fulfilling lives, new businesses, loving relationships, and healthy bodies.

What inspired you to become an entrepreneur?

It seems many people dream of becoming an entrepreneur because they hate their current jobs. This wasn't the case with me, however. I liked my corporate job. It gave me opportunities to work with various people in and outside of the company, in addition to paying me well.

I took my leap of faith because I believed I could help even more people in a more unique way. My sense of service pushed me from within. The push was quite inconvenient. I quit my job, rented out the house I'd bought less than a year prior, and moved myself from Tennessee to Oregon in October 2007. This was followed by a period of serious soul searching and business trials.

My sense of service has helped me in the long run. It always reminds me that business is primarily about helping others, about offering valuable service to those who need it. If my motivation was a self-centered one, I don't think I could have survived the embryonic phase when nothing much was happening. My sense of service also helps me to improve my offerings, which naturally results to improved customer satisfaction and more business.

Today, I have a successful practice called Akashic Record Reading, helping those who are serious about their spiritual growth. I also facilitate an intuition development coaching program. Akashic Records are great resources, forgotten by most people for centuries. I'm excited to educate people about how they can improve their lives by utilizing the knowledge of their Akashic Records.

How have you created your life on your terms?

I came to the U.S. in 1995 to rebuild my life. Back in Japan, I had a comfortable living, but internally, I was suffocated. I knew I had a higher purpose in life than just living comfortably, and I was ready to dump the comfort for my growth. My immigration brought so much new energy into my life! In two years, I completed my college education and started working again. I got married, and then divorced. I moved from Ohio to Tennessee for a job.

Somewhere along the way, I figured out that I have the power to create my life. Some people call it the Law of Attraction; some call it the power of belief. The name doesn't matter. The point is, we can envision new possibilities and create them. Or we can live as the victims of life, just letting things happen to us. The choice is up to each one of us.

I think all creation starts within. Before I quit my job, I had the vision. It was a vague vision – back then, I didn't know exactly what my new business was going to be like. But I knew I'd overgrown my role as an employee. I saw myself connecting with people of all walks of life worldwide. This vision led me to the inspired action of leaving the well-known corporate world.

I get new visions and ideas all the time. Once you start the ball rolling, it keeps going! Life feels enchanted and fun. For me, this sense of wonder is the best part of creation, beyond any specific terms about time, money, relationships, and so on.

What have you learned from mentors and role models in your life?

My mentors and role models walk into my life just at the right time. Some have been people I knew in person, some have been people I got to know through books.

One of my role models is Picasso. He achieved major success early in his life, but he didn't stop there. He kept renewing his style and stayed childlike throughout his ninety-one years of life. This is extremely difficult. Most people sit on their success once they achieve it. Picasso dared to break his own pattern. When you look at his artwork and life, it's like he lived several lifetimes in one shot. I admire his courage and ever-fresh curiosity.

Another role model I want to mention is my own grandfather. He was a physician. During the early 1940s, he was the headmaster of the Shanghai Railroad Hospital. Railroads and related businesses in China were built and run by the Japanese back then: it was part of the Japanese imperialism. So the Railroad Hospital was for the local Japanese, but my grandfather ignored this rule and took Chinese patients. This is synonymous to a German doctor taking Jewish patients during World War Two – it was outrageous and unthinkable. I'm sure he got into serious trouble with other Japanese. However, for him, the truth was plain and simple. He was a doctor and there were dying persons, so he helped them.

When I first heard this story as a child, I didn't quite understand how much it meant. Now as an adult, I'm impressed with his independent thinking, his courage to do the right thing despite his peers' disapproval, and his deep love.

Please share one tip for living a full life:

Faith. I don't necessarily mean religious faith. I mean the faith to believe in what is not there yet, and the faith that you can make it happen, even if you don't yet know exactly how.

Martin Luther King, Jr. said, "Faith is taking the first step even when you don't see the whole staircase." Without faith, you never exercise your power to create your life. And sometimes, faith is expressed in taking one inspired action toward your dream, no matter how small that action may be. In other words, even if you don't know what a full life means to you, do something toward your envisioned life, with the faith that more will be revealed, guiding you to your full life.

What would you like your legacy to be?

I want to serve as the living example that you can change your life. There may be so many obstacles, both external and internal. External obstacles are always your excuses. The truth is, we choose to be born to the family and situation that we thought would be the best learning environment for our life lessons. You are exactly where you need to be to take the next step. I know this is hard to swallow, but it's still the very first step. We need to take the responsibility to create our own lives rather than blaming our circumstances.

So, all obstacles are really internal resistance. Internal resistances are hard to catch and to work out, because we've had them for so long. But it can be done. I guess what I do in my writing and Akashic Record Reading is just that – to help people see their self-imposed obstacles and show them how to work through them. At first, this looks like a huge task, but when you start working, focusing on the root issues rather than the symptoms, things can happen quite fast.

Ultimately, my legacy is my faith in universal love. All love, including self-love, is part of that greater love.

Akemi's Message:

We can envision new possibilities and create them – or, we can live as the victims of life, just letting things happen to us. The choice is up to us. So take a step toward your envisioned life, with the faith that more will be revealed as you are guided toward fulfillment.

ARLENE BATTISHILL

"Go and be fabulous."

- Arlene Battishill

Arlene Battishill constantly has new ideas popping into her head. When she realized that the company she worked for planned to lay her off, she decided she was finally free to pursue her own ideas.

Arlene is inspired on a daily basis by things around her, both ordinary and extraordinary. She sees opportunity in everything, and loves to interact with new people because, "You never know what can happen!" She creates a life on her own terms, first, by not allowing others to determine her fate, and second, by not being held hostage economically. Believing anything is possible is a way of life for Arlene.

What inspired you to become an entrepreneur?

I'm one of those people who has a new idea every minute. It's just a matter of trying to execute it before the next idea pops in my head. When you're that kind of person, but still need to have a paycheck, it's very frustrating. You know so many things are possible, and that there's so much you can do – but you also need to have a steady source of income, so you end up feeling trapped.

When I lost my job, it was a blessing, because it forced me to live with a tremendous amount of uncertainty. I had to learn to trust that everything was going to be okay. That was a good lesson, because being an entrepreneur is much more demanding than working for someone else, and there is never any certainty. There is also no paycheck early on in the process – but there is no greater reward than working for yourself, determining your own fate, and knowing that if you succeed it will be because of your own efforts. When you work for someone else, all your effort is on the behalf of whatever company you're working for, and there is really no return on your investment other than a steady paycheck. For some people, that works, but I would rather take the risk of working for myself. Then, even if it doesn't work out, I will know that I have done everything I possibly could to create my own success.

I came up with the idea for Scooter Girls and GoGo Gear in the middle of 2008. Knowing that I was likely going to lose my job by the end of that year, I wrote a full-blown business plan and set about putting things into motion. Within two months, we were in business. It's been a whirlwind ever since!

When I left my job, I was fortunate enough to own three homes, all purchased during more prosperous years. Suddenly, I had no income, but was still carrying the mortgages on all three homes. When some people lose their jobs, they end up being paralyzed by the loss and the fear, but I felt that I was finally free. Yes, I still had financial obligations, but I wasn't going to let that stop me from pursuing something I really, truly believed in.

How have you created your life on your terms?

Number one: I will not accept someone else dictating my future. I think that the most common way that we don't live a life on our terms is because we're tied into some other person or entity economically. We sell our souls for a paycheck; we resign ourselves to give up who we are for that paycheck. But if we just do the things we feel passionate about and find a way to get paid for them, we start to live life on our own terms.

I cannot tell you how much joy I felt when I was let go from my job. I work harder now than I ever have before, but I couldn't be happier. I have a wonderful partner and wonderful friends, and I feel that as long as I am doing something I enjoy and feel passionate about, and that I feel has possibilities, then I am living the life that I want to live.

Many people go to school with the idea that they're going to become this or that. Then, harsh reality sets in when they find out what "this" actually is, but they've got too much invested to back out, and they end up miserable. I never bought into the "my job defines who I am" idea. I am probably very fortunate in the way I see things in life; I never get too attached to any one idea. If this whole Scooter Girls and GoGo Gear thing doesn't work, I'll just get started on the next idea. I don't have a huge emotional attachment to anything, and that makes it easier for me to withstand it when something doesn't work out. I don't take it personally, and I don't see it as a big catastrophe. I just think, "I need to find more money, because I'm going to start something else now." I think it makes you a whole lot more resilient, and probably more successful, when you don't have all your eggs in one basket. You say, "I'm going to throw this idea against the wall and see if it sticks. If it does, that's what I'll do, and if it doesn't, then I'll throw something else."

What have you learned from mentors and role models in your life?

I was one of the subjects for the big desegregation programs in Detroit in the mid 1970s. I was arbitrarily selected from an all-white high school and sent to an all-black high school. There were only six white people in my graduating class. One of my teachers suggested I try out for the school's golf team, and introduced me to the talent scout from the Detroit Pistons basketball team, an older black gentleman who took me under his wing and really taught me how to play golf. Three times a week, we went out to the course, and while he was teaching me the game of golf, he was also teaching me about life. He should have been the Tiger Woods of his day, but before desegregation, there were no opportunities for him. Still, he wasn't bitter. He had a long-term view of how things work in life, and where justice and fairness come into things. He had a profound effect on how I see things.

Another mentor came into the picture after my partner was diagnosed with breast cancer. As a caregiver, I not only needed assistance, but I needed to talk to somebody about my own challenges and fears. I went to talk to a woman from my employee assistance program; she started out as a therapist, but turned into more of a personal coach. She became the one person I could share things with about what I wanted to do and how I see things.

At no point did she nix any of my ideas; she always said to me, "Just go do it!" That was already my philosophy about life, but I was surrounded by people who were very practical about things – people who were not visionaries or leaders, and who were all about, "Well, how are you going to do this?" They wanted to get into the specifics of this and that, which is a major buzz kill. It is not how you do something; it's the idea itself that launches you toward where you ultimately need to go.

Please share one tip for living a full life:

You have to see opportunity everywhere. That's not just a frame of mind; it's a way of life. Most people wake up and say, "Ugh, I have to do this today." They live their lives thinking about their problems, their challenges, and all the things they have to overcome. For me, it's all opportunity. There's opportunity everywhere. You just have to reorient your thinking and recognize that opportunities are out there in abundance – but only if you're open to them. If you spend all your time focusing on what you don't have, you close yourself off to the possibility of amazing things happening.

What would you like your legacy to be?

It's more a matter of what people will say about me. I absolutely believe, without fail, that anything is possible: that's how I live. People will probably say at my funeral, "She's lying there dead, but she's probably thinking about how she can get up out of that coffin." And then they'll sit there, waiting to see if I make it happen.

Arlene's Message:

Instead of focusing on the challenges in your world, open your eyes to all the opportunities surrounding you. Release yourself from any attachment to things that keep you stuck where you are, and realize that you always have options. Once you know that everything in life is about choices, you can choose to completely change your life!

NIC ASKEW

*"I have lived on the lip of insanity, wanting to know reasons,
knocking on a door. It opens. I've been knocking from the inside."*
- Rumi

Nic is an entrepreneur because that's the only way he can be.
For him, the entrepreneurial spirit is everywhere. He is inspired
by observing ordinary people live in extraordinary ways, and by
noticing the life that runs through everything.

He has created a life on his terms by asking himself questions
such as, "How do you live a life full of space?" Or, "How do you
live with a sense of wonder?" He believes life to be a beautiful
place, although he has noted that fading eyesight can obscure
its experience.

What inspired you to become an entrepreneur?

I'm not sure I am one, at least in the usual sense of the word.
But self-invention has been a constant in my life. It has faded on
occasion, but that is less and less the case now.

I'm afflicted with a quiet curiosity for life, and for people. I
ask many questions, but have noticed that I seldom require the
answers. Perhaps that's a reasonable definition of curiosity.

I see the entrepreneurial spirit as a way in which a person could
approach life: surely the greatest entrepreneurial act is the creation
of a life fully lived. And I've noticed that, with respect to "a life
fully lived," the way a person *is* is so much more important than
what a person *does*.

As a filmmaker, I've filmed characters with magnificently dramatic
stories of overcoming extraordinary circumstance, but the stories
lost their charge, and the adventures became stories of self-
importance. There was no life running through our time together.
On the other hand, I've filmed characters that lived the most

ordinary of lives in the most extraordinary of ways, and our time together had life running through every sentence. I see these people as leading truly entrepreneurial lives – lives full of "I don't knows," of unbridled curiosity and wonder. Such lives often slip by unnoticed.

How have you created your life on your terms?

It seems to me that when you ask yourself how your life can be lived with a sense of wonder, you can live outside any imposed terms. Wonder might exist despite the things of life, but it doesn't exclude them.

I am unsure if any life based on any terms, even my own, could exist as a life in true flow. My terms seem to change often. They seem not to be able to make their minds up. I try to ignore them. Paradoxically, a life conspicuous in its absence of the usual goals seems to have allowed me to create a life without too many terms, and without the need to become someone (else) or be somewhere (else).

What have you learned from mentors and role models in your life?

I've never had a particular mentor, but everyone in my life has been a mentor in one respect or another.

I always wondered about the wisdom of wanting to be like someone else. As such, I haven't found the events of someone else's life to be inspiring in and of themselves, but that doesn't mean that they don't hold the capacity to trigger something deep inside of me. I've realized that the translation of others' events comes down to my own observation.

I enjoy encountering those who hold a light in their eyes. And I have noticed that everyone has that capacity.

Please share one tip for living a full life:

I once wrote a few words entitled "The Adventure of Uncertainty."

> "... There was a time when I looked for certainty. Certainty in the outcome of the events of my own life. And then I realized that there was only one certainty. And that was that it's all okay. That there's something that could never die. And now I realize that the total uncertainty of the events of life is the adventure. And that's the wonder."

If I had a tip, I imagine it to be hidden somewhere amongst these words.

What would you like your legacy to be?

To provoke a sense of wonder through anything I happen to have created, or left behind.

Nic's Message:

There is life running through everything. Live not for things, but live for a life full of wonder. Live so that you're forever curious. Live knowing that there is nowhere else you need to be, and no one else you need to become.

BEA RIGSBY-KUNZ

"If you are looking for a miracle, look in the mirror."
- Bea Rigsby-Kunz

Bea Rigsby-Kunz was raised in a large, strong family, and has never bought into the concept of "I can't." She is a free spirit who doesn't work within the confines of a job. After a successful career in early education, she went back to her roots to pursue a life of farming.

Bea learned very early in her first career that being a free spirit isn't always acceptable in the confines of a job. After retiring from her successful education career, she was determined to do her thing, her way – to set a new standard for herself and for her children, and take charge of the "how," "when," "where," and "if" of her life.

What inspired you to become an entrepreneur?

My inspiration came from my longing to be me – to make my own choices based on my needs and my dreams. I wanted to get out of bed in the morning and know the day was my slate; that I could design and build as much or as little as felt right.

How have you created your life on your terms?

Being true to my inner guide. Pushing forward when gravity was pulling me back. Trusting in my faith and the power it brings to sustain.

Starting a new business when you are flirting with being a senior citizen...Well, let's just say the thumbs-up, "Get out there and go for it!" reaction wasn't plentiful in coming. I heard a lot of "What if...?" and, "Are you really sure?"

There is a stigma in this society about what we are expected to do after the age of sixty. My final answer to all those doubters was, "If

I don't ask, please don't advise!" So what? I'm a radical! If I think I can, I want no one telling me I can't.

What have you learned from mentors and role models in your life?

I've had many mentors during my life. My parents taught me how to survive. A fifth grade teacher instilled the knowledge of "I'm special. No one else is like me."

During my years in education, I had a beautiful mentor in the gardening and cooking arena. Ms. Pearl was forty years older than I, and very strong and healthy. Of French/Cajun descent, she grew up on a houseboat in the swamps of Louisiana, and could garden and cook like no one I ever knew. She reinforced and added to all the basics I learned from my parents. All I know about gardening, cooking, and life can be credited to my mother Modenia and Ms. Pearl.

Please share one tip for living a full life:

Nourish your body with healthy food, and your spirit with a strong faith. Dream, even knowing that not all those dreams will come to pass; they are not meant to. They are fodder for the fields of the future, whatever may evolve into being. Never expect to make mistakes, but when you do (and you will), treat them as a gift from above, a lesson with an attached reward-knowledge. Never, ever, lose the desire to learn and try new things. Learning really is the spice of life.

What would you like your legacy to be?

I'd like to be remembered as someone who cared, loved, and worked to make every day the best it could be.

Bea's Message:

Set a standard for yourself to be in charge of your life: how, when, where, and if.

Chapter 7

Your Loved Ones

"The best and most beautiful things in the world cannot be seen or even touched. They must be felt with the heart."
- Helen Keller

In the process of conducting interviews for this project, I discovered a profound common thread which lifted my spirits: mothers and fathers are recognizing the importance of making family a priority. The understanding that we get precious little time with our children before they are grown and gone is sinking in. The almighty dollar is being pushed to the back burner, because the currency of love and family is now in first position. Financially successful people are letting go of monster careers and killer commutes in order to cultivate the riches of a healthy family.

I am grateful to be able to have breakfast with my daughter each morning, and to be available when she gets home from school most days. As an entrepreneur, I can choose to schedule my career around my life, instead of creating my life around my career. Being here for Marin is my most important job; after I tuck her into bed at night, I can work as long as I like, so there's no need for me to choose between work and time with her. The freedom to nurture myself and my family while creating a thriving business is an enormous blessing, and a significant benefit of personal liberation.

One thing I've noticed about myself since moving through my personal transition is that material things are no longer as important to me. While I still appreciate sweet cars, beautiful artwork, luxurious clothing, and travel, I've discovered that nothing compares to what you can create with your imagination – especially when you're in the company of a child who is willing to teach you about meaningful play. When I turned in my loaded SUV, I picked up a base model Subaru with a manual transmission, and fell in love with driving again. Instead of dropping hundreds of dollars to have a prized photograph matted and framed, I learned how to create my own frame using stretched canvas, craft glue, and paint. The more I allow my creativity, rather than my wallet, to provide the things I need, the more enjoyment I seem to get out of life.

The current economic climate has forced many of us to rediscover our creativity. If you're not sure where you can cut back, ask yourself, "What can I do on my own that I would normally hire out or purchase?" Tuned-in people are checking their financial "oil" by inspecting what's under the hood of their lives. It is my hope that this isn't a passing phase: that we're experiencing a new world direction where we learn to consume less and live more.

When you undertake the process of letting go of material attachments, you may notice yourself becoming more emotional or insecure. It's natural: as human beings, we often use material things as pacifiers for our deeper human needs, and when we let them go, they leave behind a question that needs to be answered, or a void that needs to be filled.

It's also important to understand that one person cannot possibly provide you with all of the support you crave and need during your transition. It's not healthy to expect your lover, spouse, mentor, best friend, or child to meet all of your expectations. It's far more beneficial to surround yourself with a select group of people who each hold part of your essence in a sacred space, and who each fill a particular "container" in your soul.

The gratitude I feel for my husband's unyielding support, my closest friend's edgy brilliance, my coach's unconventional wisdom, and my daughter's never-ending play, help me stay the course on my path to a full and meaningful life. I no longer have the time or patience for useless drama, or for people who are not supportive and primarily positive. As Michael Michalowicz states in his phenomenal book, *The Toilet Paper Entrepreneur*, "No Dicks Allowed!"

When you embrace your calling and start to love the life you live, the natural selection process of your "inner circle" may become quite interesting. When you create life on your terms, you're changing the way you relate to your world, and therefore, to the people in it. As you become your authentic self, most of your relationships will probably change for the better – but there will inevitably be a few that don't. Let them go gracefully, with compassion. Cultivating a healthy peer group is key to a successful transition. When your life is your own, there simply is no time for relationships that don't enhance your new, brighter world.

It's not difficult to tell whether your peer group is dysfunctional or healthy. If you often engage with people who take pleasure in gossip, negativity, or crazy talk, or who spend entire conversations languishing in the past, I recommend weeding your personal garden as soon as possible. What do you really gain by allowing the buzz-kills, complainers, controllers, and drama queens to hang around? They might not be "bad people" by the broader definition of the term, but their toxic energy is worse for you than you realize. People who are disinterested in self-growth will also be disinterested in *your* growth, and will tear you down when you most need to be lifted up.

Make time for introspection about your relationships, and ask yourself the following questions:

- Who do you spend your time with?
- How do they behave?
- Do you admire them?
- Do they support you?
- Where do they fit in your life?

Trusted friends and family will show up and hold a safe place for you to unfold your dreams.

If you're still struggling to identify the weeds, ask yourself this question: "If today was the last day of my life, with whom would I want to spend it?" If you answer that honestly, you've found your healthy peer group.

Why so much emphasis on relationships? Creating life on your terms is about you, isn't it? Of course! But here's a golden nugget passed down through the ages by mindful parents, teachers, and sages, and encapsulated in the following words by motivational speaker Jim Rohn: "You are the average of the five people you spend the most time with."

Your inner light will illuminate personalities that no longer suit your way of living. Don't let guilt or a sense of duty keep you from letting go of unhealthy relationships. The Law of Attraction applies even here: if you are serious about positive change, you will naturally stop engaging and attracting people who have zero interest in evolving, and begin attracting like-minded, happy people whose wisdom will help you progress. Allow the process to unfold, and watch the magic happen!

The new definition of entrepreneurship invites us not only to make a living, but to be more involved with our loved ones, and to create safer and healthier communities where we can thrive, play, and explore. The next group of interviews includes entrepreneurs whose devotion to family helped them to create new, more rewarding lives.

JONATHAN FIELDS

"Life is either a daring adventure or nothing."
- Helen Keller

For Jonathan Fields, the "professional" life comes down to the ability to create a culture by choosing the people he surrounds himself with, and having a meaningful influence on the world.

He creates a life on his own terms by striving to be present in whatever is before him. Cultivating a sense of gratitude keeps him focused on what really matters.

What inspired you to become an entrepreneur?

I didn't choose to be an entrepreneur, it chose me. Truth be told, entrepreneurship is more about the qualities I hold dear in the way I earn my living and contribute to the world than the need to be an entrepreneur. If I could find those same qualities and opportunities within an organization I didn't grow myself, I'd likely be just as happy. In the end, it comes down to the ability to create the culture, choose the people who surround me, and have a genuine impact on the world.

How have you created your life on your terms?

One of the greatest challenges for me is simply striving to be present in whatever is before me. As an entrepreneur, I'm given to aspiring to something more. It's easy to take what you have, and who's in your life, for granted. When you create intentional pauses in your day to break that cycle and create a newer, more engaged pattern, a lot starts to fall into place. Also, cultivating a sense of gratitude for what's right keeps you focused on what really matters.

What have you learned from mentors and role models in your life?

I've had a number of mentors: some of them in person, some through books, some through training. But I've yet to find that one person who gives me everything I need, and I don't think I ever will – maybe because I have an unusually broad basket of interests, or maybe because I don't feel the need to surrender myself to the tutelage of a single guru. Honestly, I've learned ten times more from my eight-year-old daughter than I've learned from any single adult expert in any field.

Please share one tip for living a full life:

Give more than you get!

What would you like your legacy to be?

I don't strive for any particular professional legacy. When I think of the word "legacy," my mind goes immediately to my family. If I've been a present, loving, giving dad, husband, brother, son and friend, that's good enough for me.

Jonathan's Message:

Create a culture around yourself that nurtures creativity and growth. Be fully present in everything you do in order to stay focused on what really matters.

Diane Helbig

"Wheresoever you go, go with all your heart."

- Confucius

Diane Helbig was inspired by her father to become an entrepreneur. Years ago, they started a business together, which was a tremendous learning experience and a prologue to her life as an independent entrepreneur. When her father passed away, she began to realize that there were things missing from her life, and that she needed to break out into something new.

Diane created a life on her terms when she realized that she enjoyed working with people who were at a crossroads in their lives. She was immediately drawn to professional coaching.

What inspired you to become an entrepreneur?

When I was growing, up my father would tell me that I could be whatever I wanted to be, as long as I was willing to do the work. He was a manufacturer's rep, and the closest thing to an entrepreneur that I'd witnessed. When I became an adult, my father asked me to help him start a business. I learned a tremendous amount from that experience – both good and bad.

Just before my father passed away, I was experiencing some difficulty at work. The owners of the company I worked for had made some decisions that were not in my best interest, and I was feeling unsettled. I had been working since I was fifteen years old with only a one-year break during my first year of college. I was a company woman – but I was also the mother of two young children, and the stress of juggling career and family was starting to wear on me. Then, my father died suddenly, and my world turned upside down.

While taking care of his estate and apartment, my sister and I talked about our lives. I shared that I felt something was missing for me. I wanted to have more of an impact in my own life, and in the universe. As the days and weeks passed, it became increasingly clear that it was time for me to break out of my life; to set a new course, and take control of my future.

How have you created your life on your terms?

Through conversations with my sister and my friends, I realized that working with people who are at a crossroads is what I like to do. It was something I did anyway in my day-to-day existence. I explored getting my Master's in counseling or becoming a coach. While listening in on an orientation call for a coaching class, I realized I had found my passion. But how was I going to head out on my own without a steady paycheck or stability?

I realized that as a salesperson I had a skill that I could offer to other companies. I could sell as an independent contractor while I was building my coaching practice. I reached out to friends who own a promotional products company, and they loved the idea.

I decided that I should also offer my services to the company I was getting ready to leave: I could stay on as a contractor and continue to earn residual commissions. At first they weren't happy with the idea, but when I told them I was giving my two-week notice, they reconsidered and we entered into a vendor/client relationship.

At the time, I felt like I was channeling my father. I was so calm, so certain of what I wanted and where I was going, that I knew I could make it work no matter what the landscape turned out to be. This income, along with some royalty money from my father's estate, provided me with the opportunity to build my coaching practice without too much financial hardship.

My husband and I cut down on some of our expenses during the transition as well. And while we had some minutes of fear, I held on to the belief that I was going to be successful, and never questioned it. Somehow I just knew this was what I was supposed to be doing.

What have you learned from mentors and role models in your life?

I've learned that the only real possession you have is integrity. As long as you act in a way that is integrity-based, you will always end up on top. People will come in and out of your life, and it is okay to decide who stays and who goes. Always be kind to others, no matter who they are: that is how you make your mark on your environment.

Remember that you never really know what is going on with someone else. So before you react, step back and assess how you want to respond. That was a big lesson for me to learn. I've also discovered that volunteering without the expectation of receiving something in return is good for the soul.

I've learned that it's important to listen to yourself. When you are overwhelmed and taking on too much, it's okay to step back and say no. At the end of the day, you are the only person who will always look out for you. Find people you can count on to remind you about what matters, and who love you enough to tell you the truth.

Finally, one of the best things I've learned is that sometimes it's good to just be quiet – to just *be*. That's a tough thing for someone like me. I'm a doer. I find it hard to sit for any period of time, but sometimes just sitting is the best thing you can do for your soul. It helps refresh you so you can dive in with more clarity.

Please share one tip for living a full life:

Be true to yourself. Too many people float through life doing what they think they should be doing. Many of them are less than happy and satisfied. You owe it to the universe to be the best you can be, and the only way to do that is to be true to yourself. Know what you want, and then devise a plan to achieve it. Don't be afraid to change course or navigate your way around obstacles. My grandmother used to say that life is long and full of wonder. She was so right! You get one go around in this body, so why not go down your own road?

Since I launched my coaching practice four years ago, I have been happier than at any other point in my life. I feel fulfilled and purposeful. I enjoy my world, and feel a greater connection to the universe. I feel I am living a fuller, more well-rounded and actualized life – and I did all this at forty-five years of age. So remember, you are never too young or too old to be the you you were meant to be. Don't be afraid: Just be you!

What would you like your legacy to be?

As I raise my children, work with my clients, and speak to audiences throughout the United States, I hope to be remembered for the ways I helped people embrace the possibilities. I'd like to be remembered for helping my clients and friends succeed – for helping them identify their potential and move toward their goals. I hope to help my children become dynamic, engaged, thoughtful, wise people who approach life with zest, interest, and a sense of humor.

I believe, as my father did, that we can be whoever we hope to be as long as we are willing to do the work.

Diane's Message:

You are never too young or too old to be the person you were meant to be. So don't be afraid: be your authentic self.

SCOTT STRATTEN

*"As you grow older, you'll find the only things
you regret are the things you didn't do."*

- Zachary Scott

Scott Stratten ventured into entrepreneurship after becoming disheartened by office politics and corporate games. With his son about to be born, he attempted to strike a compromise with his boss where he could telecommute, but his offer wasn't taken seriously. That was the last day Scott worked for someone else.

Scott has created a life on his own terms by setting professional and personal boundaries. He's learning to balance the needs of others with his own. Self-care is an important component of his success.

What inspired you to become an entrepreneur?

Other than the fact that I don't like being told what to do? I was unhappy. I was trying to create change in my workplace and kept running into dead ends. Politics, backstabbing – it was like high school, except that we got paid. I realized that there was a whole world outside my cubicle that I could work with. I also wanted to control my time, since my son was about to be born.

Since I traveled a fair bit, I told the president of the company that either I would work from home and travel as usual, or I would no longer work there. He said, "We're not ready for this telecommuting thing, so see you Monday!" I mentioned that he didn't understand what I had said. Then, I told him I was done, and left.

That was the last day I worked for someone else. It wasn't easy, but it was worth it.

How have you created your life on your terms?

Setting boundaries with my time – both for other people and for myself – has been the most important thing. When you run the show, there is no such thing as a 9-to-5, Monday-through-Friday work week. Being an entrepreneur is a 24/7/365 thing. My mind never stops, which is both powerful and horrible. I need to put the laptop down, put the BlackBerry away, and remember to focus on my family, since they're the entire reason I do all of this. Learning to say no to others and yes to myself has helped. I treat myself very well when it comes to doing things I enjoy. It might be only an hour here and there, but it works for me. You have to know how to refuel yourself under your own control, instead of relying on others.

What have you learned from mentors and role models in your life?

The traits of kindness, perseverance, and loyalty come down through the generations, and remind me daily to keep facing forward and taking one step at a time. From the inspiration of my grandparents' spirits, to my son's smile, role models are important to me – but they need to be reachable. I don't like relying on someone famous who I don't have a relationship with for inspiration. It's not victory or riches that keep me going; it's knowing how other people got to where they are that keeps me striving for something better.

Please share one tip for living a full life:

Focus on what you can control about a situation: everything else is irrelevant.

What would you like your legacy to be?

I'd like to be remembered as someone who left the world a better place than he found it – in life, in business and in his family tree.

Scott's Message:

Being an entrepreneur is demanding, but if you remember why you embarked on the journey, you will learn to set boundaries, take care of yourself, and honor the things that bring you happiness.

Susie Bedsow Horgan

"What is uttered from the heart alone,
will win the hearts of others to your own."

- Goethe

Susie Horgan was inspired to take the leap by the birth of her son. She loved her challenging high-powered job as the executive producer of *One Life to Live*, but decided she only had one son. Now, she loves being in charge of her own schedule and having time for healthful pursuits.

Her advice for living the good life is to have confidence in whatever your passion is, and believe without a doubt that you will be successful. Let yourself move forward without any hesitation.

What inspired you to become an entrepreneur?

I chose to become an entrepreneur because I was drawn to helping others. Also, I wanted to practice as a "solopreneur." I had worked for other people for many years, and longed to be my own boss and create my own work schedule without having to answer to anybody. So far, my choice continues to be very satisfying and fulfilling.

How have you created your life on your terms?

What really inspired me was my son. I was forty-three, and the executive producer of *One Life to Live*. I lived in Connecticut, more than an hour outside New York City, and I was commuting every day. I had a limousine and driver and all that to make it easy – but I was not with my son, who was five years old at the time.

It became one of those tough decisions that women have to make. It was a very high-powered job and I loved doing it. But he was my only child, so I felt it was better to set the job aside for something else.

I had written in daytime TV, so I went back to writing for *One Life to Live*. But having been in charge creatively, it was hard to go back to that, so I stopped working. I began to question what I wanted to do next. I didn't want to go back into daytime TV, because the same problem would happen again.

If I'd had a coach back then, it wouldn't have taken me so long to realize that what I really wanted to do was help people. I've always had this urge, and even thought about going back to school to become a therapist. When I mentioned this to a therapist friend of mine, she asked if I knew about life coaching, which I didn't – but I loved the name! I did some research into it, and hit upon CTI. I decided I would take the first weekend training to see if it was for me. Of course, I fell in love, and that was that. I had been in show business my whole life, and that had been exciting, but now I felt like I was forging a new career in a whole new arena.

What have you learned from mentors and role models in your life?

All the mentors in my life taught me to trust in my talents and instincts, and to follow my heart in all things. Using your heart as your North Star will always keep you exactly where you need to be.

Please share one tip for living a full life:

Have confidence in your passion, whatever it is, and have confidence that you will be successful at it. Really let yourself go without any hesitation into what it is you love to do. Believe in yourself and go forth.

As far as the day-to-day, it's wonderful to be in charge of my own schedule and be my boss. I love having that autonomy, and creating balance in my life so there's time for healthful pursuits like exercise and yoga that I never had time for before.

What would you like your legacy to be?

I would like to believe that I have made a difference in people's lives – the people I've worked with and known and loved. I would like to be remembered as someone who practiced loving kindness. My purpose in life is to open my heart to others so that they may open theirs.

Susie's Message:

Practice loving kindness wherever you go so that others will do the same. Sharing kindness inspires others to create their own successful path.

JEFF KANBAR

"Thou shalt not bullshit thyself."

\- Maurice Kanbar

Jeff Kanbar became an entrepreneur because he was passionate about his ideas. He created a life on his own terms by following his passion and trusting his gut instincts.

What inspired you to become an entrepreneur?

I don't think I, or any of the entrepreneurs I know, consciously choose to be an entrepreneur. You simply become so passionate about an idea that nothing will stop you from doing it. I was in the restaurant business, and now I'm in the liquor business: two extremely competitive fields with very high failure rates. I didn't care what the statistics were or what people were telling me. I knew if I didn't move forward, I'd regret it.

I'm mostly inspired by other entrepreneurs. I want to know how they get started and/or how they made their brand successful. It's difficult to create something from nothing, no matter who you know and how much money you have. So when somebody does it, I want to hear their story, and ask a million questions.

How have you created your life on your terms?

By simply following my passion and trusting my gut.

What have you learned from mentors and role models in your life?

My biggest role model is my uncle, Maurice Kanbar. He is an entrepreneur in every sense of the word. In addition to the over thirty-six successful patents he holds, he opened the first multiplex movie theater in Manhattan, the Quad in the heart of Greenwich

Village, and started Skyy Vodka out of his apartment in San Francisco. He looks at the world in a completely different way, and I've been able to watch and learn from him my entire life. When he uses his fork, he's thinking of a better way to make a fork – and then, he acts on it!

Please share one tip for living a full life:

Loving your work and making money at the same time is a fantastic feeling, but without health, friendships and family your life can be very unfulfilling. I know, it's pretty cliché, but it's true.

What would you like your legacy to be?

In all honesty, it would have nothing to do with business. I just want to be remembered as somebody who was loyal, honest, trustworthy, and helped others whenever I could.

Jeff's Message:

It doesn't matter what the odds are, or what other people tell you, if you are passionate about an idea, go after it!

CHAPTER 8

The Risk is the Reward

"There came a time when the risk to remain tight in the bud
was more painful than the risk it took to blossom."

- Anais Nin

In his book *Callings*, Gregg Levoy wrote, "For people cemented to the rational and scientific, the linear and observable, the ego and the five senses, opening to dreams can be extremely disquieting." Starting your own business is a monumental undertaking, and taking the risks necessary to become an entrepreneur will push you way outside your comfort zone. In other words, if you are "risk-averse," you probably don't want to become an entrepreneur.

I remember precisely when I realized I was ready to let go of everything and pursue my calling. I was in a meeting with my peers and our newly-appointed general manager. The true purpose of the meeting was lost as a discussion about the future of our sales force suddenly took a nose dive, becoming a mosh pit of ruthless madness. The experience was awful. I couldn't keep calm. My ego and my heart got caught up in the situation: I lost my cool while being interrogated by someone with absolutely zero knowledge of sales management and even less compassion for a tenured sales staff. I was trapped in the no-win game of arrogance and corporate garbage, and on the verge of an emotional meltdown.

At the moment I completely shut down, I looked out the conference room window. Blazing across the sky was an intense, perfect rainbow.

I was the only person in the room with this spectacular view, and in that instant, I knew I had to get out of the company to save my soul. Playing it safe was no longer an option. After a break in the meeting, I volunteered to fall on the sword, resign, and move on. I was done.

And then, after all that intense drama, the new general manager backpedaled to keep me on his staff. It was all just a game to him:

"Let's break the sales manager and then build her up again." I decided to stay, because the "combat pay" would allow me to move forward with my budding plans at my own pace, without forcing things. After that meeting, I endured a full year of corporate ambush meetings before I was prepared to walk the path toward entrepreneurial freedom.

My peers, close friends, and clients always had high expectations of me. On several occasions I was told that I would be the next Stephen Covey, Brian Tracy, or Louise Hay. "Shann, you have something," they would say. "You know, that thing – whatever it is." The way I see it, if it hadn't been for closed-minded people who bear no love for unconventional leaders, this "it" factor would never have come to fruition on a bigger stage. How the hell could I ever inspire anyone as a lukewarm slave to a clueless, loveless, out-of-date corporate paradigm? If it weren't for fine people like my former manager, I would still be a stressed-out sales manager living in the land of the lost.

Are you going through the motions? Are you unchallenged in your current position? If you feel even remotely like Bill Murray's character in *Groundhog Day*, you must stop selling yourself on the idea that everything is cool because you make a good living. So you live in a nice house. So your kids go to a private school. So you have stacks of cash. So what? Should you let the rest of your life slip away while you remain unmotivated, unchallenged and disrespected, simply to maintain your status quo?

For some of us, it takes a moment like my conference room rainbow experience – a moment that really smacks you upside the head – to find the kind of clarity that begs us to wake the hell up, stop lying to ourselves, and start making a difference in the world. For others, all it takes is the right question, asked at the right time. So ask yourself: "If I could do anything without fear of failure, what would it be?" Once you have an answer, begin to explore your options. What do you have to lose? There's nothing permanent or scary about being curious.

The only way to create life on your own terms is to risk moving forward. After all, without risk there can be no reward. If you're truly following your passion, you will find the courage, strength and support to see you through. Thousands, maybe millions of people have walked this path before you, believing that the consequences of doing nothing outweighed the risk of failure. Remember Alicia Castillo Holley (interviewed in Chapter 3), who arrived in Boston from Venezuela with two children in tow and just $1,400 in her pocket? Her biggest asset was her determination that she could do anything, and become anything. For her, failure simply wasn't an option.

My interview with Lorraine Edey later in this chapter proves what can happen when a person says "No more!" Edey chose to reinvent herself, and create a better life for herself and her children. Or, consider John Foote, who left a lucrative A-List career in Hollywood to pursue his passion. The examples of "risk versus reward" in this book alone are enough to excite, and there are thousands more stories out there.

The downside of taking a risk, of course, is the potential for failure. How many fortunes have been created and lost? How many great ideas never get off the ground? Most of the people in this book have failed at one thing or another in their lives. The difference is that instead of being crushed by their failures, they've chalked them up to learning experiences. Shaking themselves off, they picked themselves up and powered on, regardless of the blows they suffered.

For example, John P. Strelecky (interviewed in Chapter 1) spent his entire young life preparing to be a commercial pilot. Then, he found out that he had a rare heart condition, and his career was over before it even began. He rebounded brilliantly, setting out on an entirely new career path; then, he chucked it all and took off to travel around the world. Today, he's an international best-selling author. Who knew?

Risk-takers are ubiquitous. Look around you, and prepare to be inspired. Here are more exciting personal stories from entrepreneurs who embraced big risks to reap the rewards of personal freedom.

JOHN FOOTE

"Well, if I'm here and you're here,
then doesn't that make it our time?"
- Jeff Spicoli, *Fast Times at Ridgemont High*

John Foote considers himself fortunate to have been a kid who was raised as a kid. His mom always told him he could do anything he dreamed of, but he remembers himself as a daydreamer and a goof-off. He eventually entered the film industry, starting in the electrical department, then working his way up to the lighting department. He began to see how he could put his talents to use in the art department.

Over the years, he worked his way up the ladder and worked on many large productions and landed a job with *Mad TV* in the art department. It was the pinnacle of his career, but he knew he was being called to start his own production company. He left his A-List life and went back to Oregon to launch his business.

What inspired you to become an entrepreneur?

It seemed to be inherent to who I was. When I weighed working for someone else or myself, it seemed like a simple choice – but underneath even that, I always had these visions of things that I could do and create, and I couldn't imagine living life without creating them.

If you really want to know when I realized that running my own business was inevitable, it was when I was fifteen years old. I got a job at a local supermarket for the summer, and I worked really, really, really hard to clean the bottle counting and storage room. When I was finished, I found my supervisor and, with a huge smile on my face, I presented the bottle room to him in all its spectacular glory. His reaction was shrewd and impersonal: he said, "Yeah that's nice. Now go get that cleanup in Aisle 5!" Then, he walked off. I was completely deflated. I had expected some genuine appreciation. It was at that point I said to myself, "Man, I am going to have to run my own company if I want the rewards I'm looking for." I never forgot that experience, and I knew a day would come when I would make it happen.

Fast forward several years. I had just finished all these great indie films. I had worked with Johnnie Depp, and with HBO on the Mike Tyson story. I jumped on *Stargate*, which at the time was an $80-million feature film. Then, when I was twenty-four years old, FOX did a huge, expensive search for a handpicked crew for a new production called *Mad TV*. I made it through screening and was hired for the lead position for the art department.

But about midway through *Mad TV*, a switch went off in my head: I couldn't take it anymore. I felt that I had gone as far I could in L.A. I had to sign off and do my own thing or become an L.A. lifer. I found myself standing on Sunset Boulevard saying, "Oh my God, this is great – but horrible!" I was over the industry. I discovered that I had lost the ability to continue with the job: my heart had left it. I knew I was being called to start my own company. I packed up everything I owned and moved back to Oregon to start my own production company.

How have you created your life on your terms?

I discovered that I was capable of walking away from everything to pursue, independently, something I was passionate about. That, to this day, is so rewarding. So many people would love to be able to find the strength within themselves to walk away from what they think is security, and what they think is providing them with quality of life, in order to pursue their true passions – but they are never able to do so, or even really find what those passions might be. I was so lucky to find that.

At the end of the day, I said to myself, "If my business doesn't work out, I can always move back to Hollywood and pick up where I left off." That was really all the convincing I needed. So I packed my stuff and moved back home to Oregon to start my company and live life on my terms.

What have you learned from mentors and role models in your life?

Unfortunately, I did not have any fundamental business mentors along the way. My mom was instrumental in nurturing my belief that I could succeed at my business – or at anything in life, for that matter. Every day when I was a kid, my mom would say, "Johnny, you can do anything you want, as long as you believe in yourself and put your mind to it." That lesson has stuck with me forever. My family had no college graduates or successful businesspeople, so there was no passing of the torch, so to speak, but Mom gave me a healthy dose of self-belief, which is an amazing asset for any entrepreneur.

Please share one tip for living a full life:

No matter what you chose to do, try not to lose your perspective on who you are as a person and what to you are the important things in life, because it is easy to get lost in the ensuing madness. To me, the fundamentals of a full life are creating and maintaining involvement with the things that truly bring you joy, no matter how challenging or simple they might be; and enjoying the things you have without overshadowing them in a quest for the things that you don't have. Do not overlook, forget, or take for granted your family and core nucleus of friends. And finally, as hard as it is, live in the moment!

What would you like your legacy to be?

By the people who knew me, or knew of me, I'd like to be remembered as inspirational, fun, reliable, and genuine; a living testimony to the fact that no matter what your circumstances are, were, or could be, you can do anything you put your mind to.

John's Message:

Don't stop doing the things you love just because you're not making money at them right now. Don't get lured into the trap of a "secure" paycheck; rather, remember that there is security in your passion and talents.

LORRAINE EDEY

*"The warrior has no greater joy than to walk the path with heart.
On this path he walks, thrilled by the wonder of it all, and in
his joy he gives thanks in his heart for the marvelous privilege by
embracing everything he encounters with love and gratitude."*
                                                    - Carlos Castaneda

After being evicted from her home, Lorraine Edey decided she
would never struggle again. That paradigm shift inspired her to
enroll in college, earn her degree, and open her consulting business.

Life inspires Lorraine to move forward. She believes in trusting your
instincts and the innate calling inside you that keeps propelling
you forward to do what must be done.

What inspired you to become an entrepreneur?

At age twelve, I decided I was tired of asking my mother and
stepfather for money and getting the run around: this was the
impetus for me to start my own cleaning business. My business was
limited to the neighbors in the apartment building where I lived,
so I also hired myself out for the summers as a Mother's Helper.
I was a budding entrepreneur, convinced that I could become my
own boss and make my own money.

The women in my life were instrumental to my becoming
a "renaissance woman" and doing things on my own terms.
However, I was a late bloomer in that sense: I married at the
age of nineteen, gave birth to my son at age twenty, and had my
daughter at twenty-one.

When I was thirty, I was working in a hospital and became
fascinated with the field of social work. I decided to go back
to school. I began undergraduate studies while going through
a divorce and working two jobs. After I received my Bachelor's
degree in Psychology, I was motivated, and continued my studies

towards a Master's in Social Work at New York University.

At age thirty-eight, I began to build a psychotherapy business in New York City which promised to be highly successful and lucrative, but the entrepreneur in me was seeking a different challenge and experience, and so my next destination was Florida.

During my eighteen years in Florida, I developed a consulting and psychotherapy business. I provided training and consultation for IBM, Orlando Utilities, Bank of America, and a number of Fortune 500 companies. A new trend was developing, and I was introduced to coaching by a client. I saw it as another opportunity to provide clients with tools to enhance their lives. And so, after nearly two decades in a traditional psychotherapy business, I transitioned into coaching and reinvented myself as successful Money and Relationship Coach.

How have you created your life on your terms?

I had trials and tribulations, as well as opportunities for growth. When I was still married, and my son was small, my husband and I were evicted from our apartment. We came home one day to find that everything we owned had been taken by the sheriff. I was devastated, and sunk into a depression, I felt hopeless, lost, and defeated. I had a small child, and nowhere to live. Soon after this incident I became pregnant again, and I knew that I had to do something to get out of the dilemma I had put myself and my children into. I felt like there was something more, and I wanted it. So I divorced my husband and became a single parent.

Before I went back to school, I was employed in a variety of occupations: sales, medical and cashier. I did everything I could to care for my children, but as many single parents do, I struggled. I just could never make ends meet. There seemed to be a pattern emerging in my life, and I began to recognize it as self-sabotage.

One day, after a hard day at work, I came home to find an eviction notice on my apartment door, history was repeating itself: my children and I were going to be evicted if I did not pay what I owed immediately. I took one look at the notice and said to myself: "This is going to be the last time this happens."

There was a paradigm shift for me at that moment. I had been working hard to do better, and it was at that point that I realized that I had a choice: I didn't have to live that way anymore. That realization shifted things tremendously. That's when I decided to go back to school.

What have you learned from mentors and role models in your life?

My parents separated when I was five years old. My mother went to work, but couldn't afford to take care of my brother and I, so she sent us off to live with someone she met at the post office. My brother and I moved up to the Catskill Mountains with a family we didn't even know. This was a blessing however: the woman, who we called Aunt Lil, became our surrogate mother for about five years. From her, I learned how to cook, clean, and sew, and developed a deep spirituality.

Aunt Lil was a proactive woman, way ahead of her time. She owned a business and real estate, married late in life, and had her first child at age thirty-nine and her second at forty. She was a good role model. I learned from her the importance of living a full and balanced life, and embracing everything from a good work ethic to spirituality.

I left the Catskills at age ten and returned home to live with my mother, who was also a progressive woman: powerful and dynamic, quiet yet determined, she worked for a manufacturer of heating products for forty years. She was a representative for the Teamsters Union, and worked predominantly with men. There weren't many women at that time – in the 50s and 60s – doing what she did.

My paternal grandmother was another entrepreneur. She worked from home and developed a spiritual counseling business. Our home was always filled with people coming and going. She baked breads and sold them, and she made and sold alcohol during Prohibition. People went to her for advice; she had a wealth of information and ideas. She was truly an inspiration and model for me, as well as for the community in which she lived.

Please share one tip for living a full life:

Even when you feel fear, do not let it stop you. Fear has been a catalyst for me to grow. Trust your instincts, and the inner calling that keeps urging you to move forward.

I have a deep spiritual life and that has always been a part of my development. I trust that there is a plan in place for me. If you keep taking steps toward what you want, there's nothing that can stop you but yourself. Sometimes that may mean taking baby steps, one at a time.

Not long ago, my husband and I were looking at a place in Georgia. I love the mountains, but I have a fear of heights. The further we drove into the mountains, the narrower the roads became. We got to a point where it looked as though the road had ended. I was terrified, and begged my husband to back up and find level ground. I called the realtor we were meeting and asked him if we were still on the right road. He told me to keep going, so we did, even though I was petrified. Not long after, we came to another sharp turn, and when we rounded the bend, we were treated to one of the most majestic views in the state.

This story has become one of the metaphors for my life. If I am feeling trapped and want to stop just before the bend, I remember that if I just allow myself to keep going a little further, if I make that next turn, there will be an incredible vista.

What would you like your legacy to be?

How do I want people to remember me? I want my children to

remember me as a mother who loved them dearly, and as a woman who never gave up on her dreams. It is my hope that they too will know that they can do whatever they want to do, if they allow themselves to dream big enough.

It is my longing that those individuals whose lives I've touched can in turn be catalysts for others. We can make a difference one person at a time. I would like my legacy to be one of faith and victory. I want everyone to know that we each make a difference in this world, and I want to know that I have been a part of that difference.

Lorraine's Message:

When it looks like you can't go any further, keep moving anyway. Every step forward is a step toward your dreams and desires.

JOE MACQUARRIE

"Life is all about making choices."

\- Joe MacQuarrie

Joe MacQuarrie had a long and successful career in sales behind him when he decided he wanted more freedom. Feeling unchallenged and stagnant, he began to question why he wasn't creating and enjoying a full life. When he answered the question, "What is most important to me?" his transition from employee to entrepreneur began.

Refusing to listen to naysayers, Joe left his cushy job. He created life on his terms by defining a business environment where he works from home, without an ironclad schedule. Now, his portability allows him the luxury of travel, and he can work from anywhere in the world via his cell phone and laptop.

What inspired you to become an entrepreneur?

I became an entrepreneur so that I could better control my own destiny.

I realized I was turning into a person I wasn't happy with. The 9-to-5 job was no longer satisfying my needs. Punching a clock for someone else is not what life is about for me. I wasn't getting any younger and I had always wanted to have my own business.

It took a couple of years to realize that I was losing myself; I was making really good money, but my life was not of the quality that I wanted. I began to wonder, "Why do I have to live by these rules? Why do I have to sit in an office even when I've exceeded all my goals? Why do I have to be tied down to exactly three weeks of vacation a year? Why do I have to be boxed in by all this?"

When I decided to leave, I was under a lot of stress from political garbage, and knew it was the right time to make a positive change.

The first thing I did was to come up with a list of names for my company. Then, I started jotting down prospect ideas, and outlining how I was going to make money. Then, I put my notice in.

A lot of people thought I was absolutely crazy. They were thinking, "You've got a house, a motor home and three cars – how on earth are you going to do it?" I was bringing in a six-figure income and doing very well at my job, but I wasn't happy, so I didn't care! I had eight months of income and funds I could draw from to pay the bills. I had booked a cruise for my parents' 50th anniversary three months after I left my job, and I didn't even cancel it. I knew my plan was going to work.

How have you created your life on your terms?

I refused to listen to the people who told me, "Lots of people have tried to do that, and they weren't successful." I didn't listen to people who said I was going to fall on my face, or lose my house. "I'm going to make it," I thought.

The most important thing about my business plan was that it was constructed around my needs and interests. My dream was to have a business that did not require me to go to an office every day. I did not want to have show up somewhere on a schedule: I wanted to be portable. So I figured out how I could run my business from anywhere in the world using a laptop and a cell phone. Occasionally I have to meet with clients, but I don't set up that expectation. They're busy and I'm busy. I do what they need me to do, and they're happy.

What have you learned from mentors and role models in your life?

I have had many mentors who have inspired me over the years. No single person has ever been my mentor per se: rather, the combined traits of many people have helped to create a vision of a perfect mentor in my mind.

Please share one tip for living a full life:

Think about your dream life. How would you like to live your life on a daily basis, a weekly basis, a yearly basis? What's important to you? Once you know that, work backwards toward your dreams and goals. Ask yourself what you could begin doing to make your dreams a reality.

What would you like your legacy to be?

I would love for people to remember how much I enjoyed my life and my relationships, and to remember the love I shared with friends and others around the world. I want them to say, "Do you remember how crazy he was? He took three hundred cruises in his lifetime!"

When it's all said and done, do you want your epitaph to note what a good worker bee you were? Should it read, "He never took a sick day, and always showed up at the office?" NO! My epitaph will say: "Experienced the world. Understood the world. Treasured his relationships."

Joe's Message:

You don't have to be boxed in by the rules of society. It doesn't matter how crazy your dream is, or what other people think of it. Begin to plan and create your greatest life today.

LINDA JOY

"To come to be you must have a vision of Being, a Dream, a Purpose, a Principle. You will become what your vision is."
- Peter Naive

Linda Joy's journey into entrepreneurship has been one of self-discovery. She's learned to follow her heart and her passion, and has found a way to provide a service which both empowers others and aligns with her own ideals. She maintains that letting go of the outcome, trusting in the process, having faith in your choices, and listening to your inner wisdom are the best ways to discover a life on your own terms, and keep moving forward no matter what curveballs life tosses your way.

What inspired you to become an entrepreneur?

"Inspired" is a great way to describe my journey. Looking back over my seventeen years as an entrepreneur, I realize that I never actually intended to start a retail business, become an event producer, or launch a magazine – although I did all of those things. In each instance, I just followed my heart, my passion, and my calling to provide a service that could empower and inspire women. By the act of living each day doing what I fully love, my businesses were born through what I can only describe as an organic process.

I passionately believe that each of us has a calling in our hearts and a unique gift to offer the world, and that if we take the time to do the inner work and align with our purpose, the Divine takes over, and will move mountains to bring our gift to us.

My evolution from welfare mom to award-winning entrepreneur took twenty years, and despite all of the ups and downs, the successes and failures, I can honestly say that the journey has been worth it. It has been an amazing process of self-discovery. I know things will only get better as I continue to live my truth, trust in myself, and let my purpose lead me forward.

How have you created your life on your terms?

Creating life on my terms is a journey, an unfolding: each new experience, in business and in life, adds to the knowledge and wisdom I may use in tomorrow's decisions. Living life on my terms has meant learning to let go of the outcome, having faith in my choices, and listening to the innate inner wisdom that I believe we all possess. It means living authentically and allowing myself to be vulnerable and trusting, stepping out of the box, and living each day with an open heart, no matter what curveballs life throws my way.

What have you learned from mentors and role models in your life?

Books have always been my greatest teachers. Since childhood, I have been an avid reader and seeker. For many years, books were all I had access to for inspiration, and the wisdom they contained helped me uplift and transform myself from a welfare mom into an entrepreneur.

The written word has always been a powerful catalyst for me, and continues to be. I giggle at times because now, as a publisher, I am bringing inspiration to women across the globe. It is my hope that the words of our *Aspire* contributors touch these women as others' words have touched me.

A few years ago, I realized that I am constantly surrounded by amazing women – both personally and professionally – and so I started to reach out to bring them together. Whether I was holding intention groups at my home, producing inspirational events, or bringing women together for *Aspire's* Advisory Board, I surrounded myself with the wisdom of these powerful women. Each has brought their own unique wisdom, gifts, and insight to the table, and all of them have been instrumental in inspiring, guiding and encouraging me.

Please share one tip for living a full life:

Live your life, not someone else's idea of what your life should be. Uncover your unique gifts and bring them out into the world. Tune into what brings you joy, as this is the key to discovering your purpose. Each day, step out of your head and into your heart, and just listen. It is never too late to begin anew.

What would you like your legacy to be?

I would like to be known as a Spiritual Entrepreneur who showed others that it is possible to lead from the heart, and create a conscious, successful business without compromising your dreams or ideals.

Linda's Message:

Embrace the journey you are on, learn from the lessons that have come your way, and live an inspired life!

CHAPTER 9

Discover Your Groove

"People often say that this or that person has not yet found himself.
But the self is not something one finds, it is something one creates."
- Thomas Szasz

I was a new mother when I realized it was time for a change of metamorphic proportions. Somehow, I had misplaced my creativity, and gotten lost in the roles I'd created (which I'd lived up to swimmingly). No longer content to bump around in my day-to-dayness, I took action and enrolled in a martial arts class, studied professional coaching, and became a student of Yoga. Creating a well-balanced and fulfilling life meant making room for new activities that piqued my curiosity.

As human beings, we have limited time to explore, create, and uncover our passions. The need to follow my bliss became clear with time and cerebral "cave spelunking" introspection. I realized that I am on the earth to inspire people in transition, and to help them reach their full potential. I was meant to do something more than manage a sales force for a paycheck; something more than just stave off the corporate soul-suckers.

Discovering that professional coaching was a viable new profession for me lit me up like Times Square! After reading *Co-Active Coaching* by Laura Whitworth, Henry Kimsey-House and Phil Sandahl, I was immediately hooked. This coaching guide opened my eyes to new methods of inspiration, support, and leadership. I quickly included coaching practices in my corporate leadership role. Suddenly, there was a new, healthier energy flowing in the sales department. Twelve months after implementing the new leadership style inspired by *Co-Active Coaching*, we had our best selling year ever!

Discovering these powerful coaching tools helped me hone my intuition, and breathed new life into my career for about three years. At the three-year mark, however, the economy was starting to spit and sputter, and the owner of the television station appointed a new general manager. (Remember the mosh pit incident from Chapter 8?) After that, it didn't take long to see that I no longer belonged with the organization.

Evenings, weekends and lunch hours became dedicated to awareness, personal development, and studying for my professional coaching certification. The plan was to build my coaching business and the True Balance brand a little at a time, until I could give my two weeks' notice and say farewell to corporate life.

Moving forward and creating your new path involves asking yourself meaningful questions like:

- What are your strongest beliefs about yourself and the world right now?

- What gifts do you have that you would like to make available to the world?

- When in your life did you feel most creative?

- What are the greatest accomplishments in your life to date?

- What is the most important life lesson you have learned so far?

Answering these thought-provoking questions helped me navigate the choppy waters of my career transition. The secret is to have the courage to sit with yourself long enough, and be honest enough, to figure out how you can best share your talents with the world. Some of the best advice I've ever received, and which I share to this day, is to stay light, and not take yourself too seriously.

Less than two years later, I was ready to claim my liberation. The choice to leave my powerful position with the television station and start over with a clean slate as an inspirational entrepreneur is the most rewarding professional decision I have ever made.

The first full year on my own felt surreal. The process of reprogramming my brain to step into my role as a coach and entrepreneur was exciting. For the first time ever, I was responsible for creating my world as I wished. I was optimistic and freaked out at the same time. I was hungry to make the best use of my time while enjoying the fact that I had nobody to answer to but myself and my new clients.

I felt a bit like an artist sitting before a clean white canvas, playing a round of Beat the Clock. I was totally immersed in the tasks which needed to be accomplished to get my new business up and running. I worked my ass off for the first ninety days. My transition had proven that there was nothing I could not accomplish, so I figured I would condense three years of work into three months, and create a healthy, profitable business overnight.

Then, I got a wake-up call.

A serious car accident and a couple of broken ribs told me the universe was sending me a message to slow down. Growing my business would take time, I realized, as well as concentrated effort. I had not left corporate America to burn out in my first year as a solopreneur!

From the accident came a deep understanding that I could walk my talk and create a full and balanced life on my terms. Now my business is orchestrated to complement my natural rhythms. I choose a life where work is play – and my particular brand of play is my life, lived with joyous abandon. To make this possible, I have implemented a solid organizational structure and back-end system, and assembled a group of talented professionals to help me carry the weight of each new venture. I would not be where I am today without the investment, expertise and kindness of each of these brilliant minds.

Now, I keep my business organized and on track by using an electronic business calendar and a Moleskine™ planner to designate time for clients, marketing, writing, accounting, and personal pursuits.

The value of hiring a dynamite coach to champion me in the discovery of my authentic self and business niche cannot be quantified. My first mentor/coach was like an archeologist, and I the ancient artifact encased in lifetimes of sediment: I felt like I was just waiting to be gently uncovered, carefully brushed off, and finally revealed as my authentic self. Discovering and sharing my true Shann-ness is one of the keys to my happiness and success.

A realistic and organized game plan, along with support from my coach, mentors and peers, has allowed me to acquire a professional coaching certification, open two new businesses, earn my Yoga teaching certification, coauthor a best-selling book for women, create Luscious Living Play-Shops, co-create AnxietySlayer.com, and interview extraordinary entrepreneurs from all over the world for this book. I share my time and talent inspiring creative entrepreneurs and powerful women in career transition to accelerate life on their terms and create balance in their lives through coaching, yoga, and creative expression.

I'm living the dream at last, and I created it on my own terms. Metamorphosis complete.

Check out more examples of courageous people who left the conventional world behind...

LAURA LOPEZ

*"Our chief want in life is somebody who shall
make us do what we can."*
- Ralph Waldo Emerson

After working in corporate America for twenty years, Laura
Lopez discovered that she was no longer fulfilled by the corporate
environment, and began to feel a shift in her priorities. Soon
after, she made time to pursue a serious relationship, and
eventually adopted a baby. She began to draw parallels between
parenting and corporate management, which led to her writing a
book entitled *The Connected and Committed Leader: Lessons from
Home, Results at Work*.

What inspired you to become an entrepreneur?

I became an entrepreneur so that I could express the multifaceted
person that I am, and as a result, have a bigger impact on people
and their lives. I always believed that if I could bring all of myself
to work, that there would be no limit. I spent over twenty years
in corporate America, and gained many skills. As a VP with the
Coca-Cola Company, I achieved a high level of success. However,
during that time, I felt that there were many aspects of myself that
I checked at the corporate door. I always yearned to have my own
business where I could bring together so much more of who I am.
I never knew what it would be, but I had faith that one day the
opportunity would present itself, and it did.

How have you created your life on your terms?

My life really started to change after I turned forty. I was reevaluating
many things at that time. I had a big and demanding job, and
although I was single and didn't have a family life to juggle, work
wasn't working for me, and it wasn't allowing other aspects of my
life to work either. I really was unhappy.

It all started to change when I started to live my priorities. I started cutting back on travel and working fewer hours so that I could meet someone. Four years later, I was well into a serious relationship and we were starting the adoption process to start a family together. Our daughter Leila came into our lives in March 2005. She was eleven months old at the time. She sparked something inside of me that has become the catalyst for creating my life on my terms. She taught me the true meaning of leadership, and inspired me to write a book. As a late-in-life mom, I realized that parenting is not much different from leading people at work, and vice versa. My book, *The Connected and Committed Leader: Lessons from Home, Results at Work*, led me to leave my corporate job and launch my business as a speaker, trainer, and coach. Now I work from home, inspiring others through my experiences and helping thousands of women to realize that skills learned at home can serve them at work, and vice versa.

What have you learned from mentors and role models in your life?

The best mentoring I ever received was unappreciated at first. I had a boss who was trying to steer my career out of marketing and into Human Resources. I resisted because I wanted to excel in line management, but he knew where my passion was, and that was in the people business. It wasn't until years later that I realized he was right. My natural strengths lie in developing insights around human behavior. In my current work, I use these skills more than I ever did in line management.

The great thing about mentors is that they can see things you can't always see for yourself. It is important to be open to the views that others have of you.

Please share one tip for living a full life:

Ensure that the choices you make are aligned with your values and goals. If you are in alignment, then the choices you make will take you down the path toward a full life. Unfortunately, we often make choices that are out of alignment because we haven't taken the time to really understand our personal values and goals. Instead, we pursue choices that support our parents', family's or friends' values and goals for us.

What would you like your legacy to be?

I would like to be known as an advocate for women in all aspects and areas of life. I support women developing and growing as multifaceted beings, and believe that we should never be ashamed or afraid of being anything or anyone – especially of being mothers. The skills we learn as mothers make us stronger leaders and businesspeople.

Laura's Message:

Embrace the many facets of your life, and never apologize for the path you choose to take. Live your life according to your values, and integrate your skills in a positive way – whether they're learned in a boardroom or in your own home.

LYNETTE CROW

*"Life is not about waiting for storms to pass,
it's about learning to dance in the rain."*

- Anonymous

Lynette Crow doesn't feel that she became an entrepreneur; rather, she was born one. Once she succeeds at starting a new business, she immediately wants to start all over again. She is inspired by creating companies that bring good people together and create good jobs.

For Lynette, life on her own terms is about working hard and treating people well. She loves giving back to her employees, and making people feel appreciated. She credits her success to her technique of working backward from her end result.

What inspired you to become an entrepreneur?

I believe that you either are an entrepreneur, or you are not. I have always been curious about how entrepreneurial people do what they do. I have always been into self-help books and motivational behavior.

I purchased my first home at the age of twenty-three; I assumed a VA loan even though I had no job. I started with the end in mind, and was able to pick up a very nice home in a neighborhood with good resale values for only the amount that was owed on the mortgage. I was able to get all the first-time home buyer perks, knowing I would have instant equity.

This is how I have lived my life: I jump on opportunities, and see where they take me. I get bored once a business I have created is up and running, so I have the need to do it again and again. I love taking business to the next level; this is what drives me.

I am inspired when I see things come together for the good of all. I love creating new companies because new companies create good jobs for good people. I love being able to give back, and watch my businesses evolve to profitability for the good of everyone involved.

How have you created your life on your terms?

Work hard, always do a good job no matter what the job is, and finish what you start. If you borrow something from someone, always return it in better shape than it was when you borrowed it. These are the particular standards to which I was raised, and which have shaped everything in my life – from raising my children, to building my businesses, to growing my garden. I never expect anyone to do a job I wouldn't do. I always treat people how I want to be treated. I love to give: nothing makes me happier than buying someone a gift for no reason at all – especially someone who's feeling under-appreciated. No matter what business I am involved in, or what project I am working on, I adhere to these principals. You have to work hard, but you have to appreciate people along the way.

What have you learned from mentors and role models in your life?

In hindsight, I realize that my mentor was my late husband. I had no idea how much I relied upon his knowledge, his common sense, and his opinion, until I didn't have it anymore. He'd had a job since he was fifteen years old, paid cash for his first car when he was seventeen, and spent five years in college to earn a business management/computer degree. I watched him grow from a young man right out of college making $10.00 per hour, to becoming the youngest VP in a Fortune 500 Company. He accomplished it all with hard work, good standards, and good decisions.

Please share one tip for living a full life:

Life is not about waiting for the storm to pass: it's about learning to dance in the rain. Everyone these days has so many problems, it seems. People deal with depression, marriage issues, kids on drugs, and elderly parents. They can't get a job, or they don't like their boss… The list goes on and on, but life really is what you make of it.

If you choose to stay stuck in excuses, and keep telling yourself the same sad story every day, nothing will ever change for you. In fact, it will get worse. I am not saying depression isn't a real disease, but I believe it is a mindset as well. Positive self-talk is very important for success. If you tell yourself you are successful, you are! It is really that simple.

My husband of seventeen years committed suicide. After some research, we discovered that his depression was chemically induced by the use of illegal steroids sold in third world countries. Needless to say, this came completely out of the blue, and steroid use seemed completely out of character for my husband. The shock factor was unbelievable. Once I realized what had happened to my life, I knew that I had a choice: I could lie down, make all of the excuses that would seem perfectly normal to those around me, and fall apart; or, I could pick myself up, and turn this terrible tragedy into positive energy. I still had one daughter at home who was a senior in high school; the other started college two weeks later. I had to be a strong role model for these girls, who were going to hurt for the rest of their lives. I made the decision to go on – to be stronger and better and kinder to everyone in my path in my husband's name. It wasn't easy, but it really was a choice.

What would you like your legacy to be?

I would like people to say that I loved people like Jesus loves people: unconditionally. That I cared about people and about what happened to people, and that I made a difference in their lives. That I was able to help people become stronger, better, more independent, and more confident, and teach them that if we all do our part to give back, our world becomes a better place.

Lynette's Message:

Make the decision to be stronger, kinder and more positive. A full life happens when you cultivate a positive mindset and contribute to the success of others.

Michael Michalowicz

"Passion begets persistence, and persistence begets success."
- Michael Michalowicz

A former employee at a computer store, Michael Michalowicz became an entrepreneur at the tender age of twenty-four, after he got tired of working for The Man. He quit his job without knowing what his next step would be – but thanks to his thirst for success, his willingness to be completely real, and his staunch adherence to his four "immutable laws," he's catapulted himself into the national spotlight with his book, *The Toilet Paper Entrepreneur*, and his third company, Obsidian Launch.

What inspired you to become an entrepreneur?

The reason I became an entrepreneur was not traditional. I didn't grow up wealthy, and I didn't grow up poor with something to prove. We were a total Beaver Cleaver, middle class family.

I'd never had an ounce of interest in becoming an entrepreneur, but one night, after finishing work at the computer store, I went out for a couple of beers with a coworker. After throwing back four or five cold ones, I said, "Screw this, I'm not working for The Man anymore. He's not even that smart. He's probably a multi-millionaire of off my sweat! I'm quitting and starting my own business." My friend replied, "Well, if you've got the guts, do it now."

I'd made my announcement in a drunken stupor, but it turns out I did have the guts: hung over, I resigned the next morning. I was twenty-four, married, and had a three-year-old son. The job I'd just left was the only one I'd had since I'd gotten out of college. I came home that day to my wife and son and said, "Good news, bad news. The good news is, I think we're gonna be rich. The bad news is, I have no idea how, and I just quit my job."

It was pure panic the first year or two, just surviving. Initially it was the fear of failure that drove me; later, it became the thirst for success. There was a lot of sacrifice. I had a young family, no savings, and now, no salary. We were renting an apartment we could no longer afford. Our parents were not excited about us moving home, nor did we want that ourselves. The day I quit my job, I told my wife she had to find us someplace to live that was really cheap and safe for our son. She found a retirement village that we lobbied to get into, and for a year we lived with people in their eighties and nineties.

How have you created your life on your terms?

Necessity really is the mother of invention. I always thought you needed money to make money, but now I emphatically believe that the lack of money incites ingenuity, passion, and persistence, and those are what make real money. I started becoming inventive in many ways. I would do marketing stuff, which takes no money. People actually pay me to help them with their marketing now, because I come from the mentality of "How can we do it without any money?" My company, Obsidian Launch, specializes in helping new entrepreneurs learn how to grow healthy businesses.

The biggest guiding principal – and this is the bedrock for building a life on your terms – is discovering and then defining your laws. I don't say "values," because the term is so used and abused by corporations. But we have our own core values: we know what they are the moment we break one of them, because we feel sick to our stomachs and think, "I can't believe I did that." Other times, people are shocked because you've declined an "opportunity," but you feel really good anyway, because you adhered to one of your immutable laws.

I discovered my four immutable laws early on. They're clearly defined: I have them on my wall, and I look at them every morning. They have become the standard filter. Documenting them, and living them religiously and emphatically, has helped me recognize the "sacrifices" that will actually become gains in the long term. One of them is "No Dicks Allowed." I will never be a dick to someone else. If someone is a take-take-take person, I have no interest in dealing with them. When I'm hiring an employee, I'm not just asking what his or her background experience is; I'm asking questions to find out what kind of person they are. "Are you a dick?" I ask, "Or not a dick?" I've turned down what I considered big deals, because the manager on the client's side was a dick. Although I'm losing out on a lot of money, I'm gaining a lot of life. To work for someone who's a total dick is so draining!

My other three laws are: "Give to Gift," "Positivity or Death," and "Blood Money." You'll hear people say "give to get." But then, when you give something, you're assuming you're going to get something: you're going into it with a "taker" mentality. It's a bit dickish, actually. If you don't want to give for the joy of giving, then you're really not giving – you're just trying to manipulate getting.

Next is "Positivity or Death." I've found that people are wired to be half-empty or half-full when they see that glass, and you can't teach anyone to see it the other way. I constantly seek out people who see the positive side, even in dark situations.

The final immutable law is "Blood Money." Money shouldn't be treated like water or urine, so don't piss it away. Your cash flow is the blood of your business, and without it, you're dead. You have to treat money with respect, and you have to use it in a disciplined way. A savings account is like a blood bank: you should keep a reserve of money for an emergency situation, whether your own or a colleague's, and you should always be building that blood reserve, because you never know when that life-or-death moment will hit.

What have you learned from mentors and role models in your life?

When I first started my company, I was under so much stress. Someone recommended that I read *How to Stop Worrying and Start Living* by Dale Carnegie. I thought a book couldn't help me, but what a powerful book! That was my first experience with a mentor, even though Mr. Carnegie had passed away fifty years prior.

Currently, I have three mentors, and I'm looking for a couple more. I always start with the categories where I think I need the most progress. I believe that right now there is a major surge in terms of women becoming entrepreneurs, to the point where in ten years, we won't be saying, "The next Bill Gates," we'll be saying, "The next Barbara Gates!" Women are going to take over the leading roles. I have lots of arguments to support this, and beyond just believing it, I'm behaving that way. One of my most important mentors is Nancy Devine. She's an entrepreneur, but also a spiritual and strong woman. She's gone through some big challenges in her life and has come out very successful and positive. For me to live the belief I have, I have to entrench myself in it. I meet with her once a month for a cup of coffee and just soak in every single word and experience she's gone through.

Howard Hirsch is a mentor too. He's in an investment company, he's part of the "No Dicks Allowed" belief, and he constantly drives home the value of his company. The guy is not money first: money is fifth with him. Instead, the customer is first; then, being true to who you are, integrity, and ethics. After these, the money is automatic.

Frank? He just happens to be my long-lasting mentor; he's worked with me for fifteen years. From the first day I became an entrepreneur, he was there. He's all about business discipline.

Finally, I'm in a mastermind group – a whole group of mentors. My group includes eight other entrepreneurs and we've been meeting for eight years. Everyone in the group has something I don't have. There's one guy I really admire for his fathering skills: he's extraordinary. There is another person who went through challenges with alcohol, and has overcome that. I've never experienced that, but we all struggle with an addiction of some kind, and her experience is so powerful.

Please share one tip for living a full life:

Unequivocally, it is being yourself. Many of us still pander to what we think society wants or expects of us. I did it too: I was constantly pushing myself down so I wouldn't stand out, or embarrass myself. I was always comparing what I wanted to do with how my wife wanted me to behave, how my parents raised me, what my friends would think of me.

I've had three companies, but it was only with my most recent company that I said, "Fuck it. I'm me! Why not just be me?" I put the real me out there and the result has been overwhelming, tremendous, and fulfilling for me and my business. A year ago, I didn't have a book, and I didn't have a web site. But just by being myself I became this soapbox person – the kind of person people look at and say, "Holy shit, there's someone that says what I think. I like that!" When people connected with me, it was great for business, but internally I was so relieved. I thought, "My God, all this time, all I had to be was me? How bizarre!"

What would you like your legacy to be?

It changes. I don't know that I legitimately have a legacy yet, but at the moment, I want to change the entrepreneurial frontier. Right now, I'm taking my stance: I do not believe in get-rich-quick, and I don't like when people try to take advantage of other people. Turn on the TV at 10:00 p.m., when the infomercials kick in, and it's like, "Are you desperate? Well, here's your salvation!" Then, it's, "Give me ten thousand dollars and you'll get a million dollars!" They're going to take your money because they're scammers. The great irony is that they're scammers with huge amounts of wealth behind them.

I don't believe in get-rich-quick. I believe in get rich right, and the "right" is determined by all those things we discussed earlier – your immutable laws. I'd like to deliver that legacy to women entrepreneurs. They are positioned so well right now to take off, but they have a challenge that men don't, and that is that women analyze much more than men. I see a lot of women who are ready to become entrepreneurs, but they get into an over-think process, and stonewall themselves before they ever get started.

Mike's Message:

Be yourself. You don't have to work with or surround yourself with anyone who devalues your own belief system. Don't try to get rich quick: live by your immutable laws to get rich right.

WILL WILKINSON

"There is nothing like a dream to create the future."
- Victor Hugo

Will Wilkinson won't be confined to working a traditional job: his imagination is far too active. He is compelled to use his creativity as an entrepreneur. He is inspired by anything that contributes to awareness of the shared challenges of the human condition.

Will lives as though every moment is an adventure. He has embraced transformation as the core of his life, and tries to absorb and accept change without reservation.

What inspired you to become an entrepreneur?

As a born innovator, it is confining for me to have a "regular" job. My imagination continually creates new things to work and play with. Becoming an entrepreneur was not a decision, but simply a natural way for me to be in the world. Also, I have always enjoyed tracking the connection between ideas and results – something that is necessary as an entrepreneur, but not so much on the assembly line.

I'm inspired by any expression of passion and originality, both in real time and in art. There is a tangible feel to anything that is made by someone who is a real creator; that is, someone who is motivated by the urge to create, and not just using their skills to make a living.

I am also inspired by anything that probes deeply into the human condition in a way that illuminates our shared challenges while underlining our synergistic qualities, and by anything that brings evidence of the divine into user-friendly forms. Music, art, movies, poetry, sparse but penetrating prose: anything that casts its spell from a place of genuine contribution inspires me.

How have you created your life on your terms?

An astrologer told me that I am destined to live as though I am on the prow of a ship heading into unknown waters. So, I create life as an adventure, and do my best to feel into every moment of it. Since my very nature dictates that I will constantly be experiencing newness, building, then letting go, I have embraced transformation as the core theme in my life. Over the years, I have learned to go with the flow, and to trust that something even more rewarding than what I am losing is about to peek around the corner and get my attention.

What have you learned from mentors and role models in your life?

I have had a string of mentors, beginning with a crazy high school English teacher who nurtured my passion for writing. Anwar Sadat was a light, and I wept when he was killed. John Lennon, what a wild card: similar lousy fate. I had a spiritual mentor for over twenty years who gifted me with both wisdom and wounds which, as I have healed them, have given me a more compassionate access to others.

My father, who died several years ago at age ninety, taught me carpentry. He also showed me how radically a person can change in their last years, giving me hope that when I near my end I will also become more loving with others.

Please share one tip for living a full life:

A life fully lived is counted in moments. Embrace each one, and absorb it deeply, without reservation. We can learn to be present, facing what are often brutal facts in our current reality, while simultaneously energizing our vision of what we want.

I believe this is the secret to creating a real life: the ability to hold the two poles of current reality and passionate vision, feeling the pulsation of life force that moves in the structural tension between them; then, to track actions towards results and heal whatever blocks and wounds arise along the way.

And, to exorcise the demons of underdeveloped self esteem, there is nothing like celebrating small successes. Completion, when ritually acknowledged, releases a special energy that seeds our next creations. This works for nature, and it works for us! Harvest brings not only fruit but seeds. The more I learn to leverage what I have just created into what naturally comes next, rather than just making up something disconnected (and with my imagination this requires constant monitoring), the easier my life gets.

What would you like your legacy to be?

I'd like to be remembered as a kind person. I will leave a few books, some buildings, courses, etc., but my real legacy will be the memories that my family and friends have of me. Hopefully these will be memories of a fun guy with occasional wisdom and full-time availability, someone who dove into his humanness from a high place, without fear that this might contaminate him or prevent his eventual return.

Will's Message:

Learn to go with the flow, and allow yourself to naturally transition through life. Absorb each moment fully, learn from it, celebrate or heal, then let it go and move forward.

CHAPTER 10

Creating True Balance: Living the Dream

"To dream anything that you want to dream. That's the beauty of the human mind. To do anything that you want to do. That is the strength of the human will. To trust yourself to test your limits. That is the courage to succeed."

- Bernard Edmonds

The process of becoming a new business owner can feel all-encompassing. It can grab you by the tail and spin you about, leaving your head whirling and your stomach a little queasy. In order to keep taking steps forward, you need time to recoup, get your bearings, and get your feet back under you. Being aware of what your mind, body and spirit need to function is not only essential to living a full and healthy personal life, it's essential to business success.

As I mentioned in Chapter 9, building your business is an incremental process. Every "overnight success" has a significantly longer back-story. Of course, diligent work will be necessary to create your new life, but pushing yourself to the point of burnout is not a guarantee of success. Creating a well-balanced entrepreneurial reality involves knowing how to ease your mind, calm your body, and feed your soul, so you can approach each day with verve and curiosity.

Easing your mind begins with being fully present and aware of *this* moment. Learn to eliminate any guilt and shame you carry with you from your past, and put an end to unfounded worries about your future. Now is the time to create gratitude, abundant thinking, a positive attitude, and heaping servings of laughter.

Here are some ways to put your mind at ease, and cultivate positive mental/emotional habits.

- Create a gratitude journal: Start making a daily list of what you are grateful for.

- Start Joy-Spotting: Notice every little moment that fills you with joy.

- Read motivational books, magazines, and blogs.

- Listen to uplifting music, podcasts, and audio books.

- Be aware of your self-talk. Be gentle and kind to yourself.

- Lighten up! Things do not have to be so frigging serious!

- Look at who you are sharing your time with. Do they make you laugh?

Easing your mind is vital to your mental and physical health, but exercise and relaxation also play a key role in your well-being. Our bodies are marvelous creations that carry us through life. You deserve focused self-care. Like a beautiful flowering plant, your body needs rich soil, fresh water, and healthy, nutritious food to fully bloom.

Care and feeding instructions for your healthy body:

- Invest in bodywork. Regular massage therapy should be part of your health care routine.

- Take relaxing baths. If you have a tub, get in it!

- Enjoy luxurious naps. You deserve at least one per week.

- Get moving! Walking, yoga, gym time, running, stretching, and playing can all help burn stress and bust tension.

- Be kind to yourself. Banish negative body talk. Learn to cherish your body as the vehicle for your mind and soul.

- Cultivate a healthy diet: Plenty of water, fresh fruit, vegetables, and whole foods are vital to radiant health – like premium gasoline for your internal engine.

Discovering true balance includes creating time to feed your spirit. Spiritual nurturing allows you to ground yourself in your body, keeping you anchored, healthy, and alive. Caring for the soul includes eliminating the weeds of self-sabotage that pop up to choke your natural grace. You deserve to create quiet time for thoughtfulness and reflection.

Some easy ways to nourish your soul:

- Banish interruptions, and make time to be still.

- Get in touch with your spirituality through peaceful time in prayer or meditation.

- Create time for creative pursuits like photography, journaling, art projects, and music.

- Unplug: Turn off the TV, radio, computer, pager and cell phone.

- Focus on your breath. Take a deep cleansing breath in through your nose, filling your lungs to capacity; then, let it all out with a giant sigh. Repeat five times or more.

- Share your time with people who make you smile until your face hurts.

- Get out of the office and get close to nature. The miracles of water, woods, and wildlife will rejuvenate your spirit.

When you give a big chunk of your energy to enterprise, you need real moments of solitude, self-reflection, play, and relaxation to balance out that expenditure. After all, you only have so many units of get-up-and-go in your internal checking account, and in order to have energy to spend, you need to replenish. Curiosity, courage, and self-care are investments, and their returns are manifold and amazing. When you acknowledge that *you* are the most important asset to your business, any guilt you're harboring about making time for self-care will vanish.

Read on to discover how our final group of inspirational entrepreneurs created full and balanced lives on their terms.

- What are you most curious about?

- What thoughts can you let go of that no longer suit you?

- What do you like to do for rest and relaxation? How often do you do it?

- What action will you commit to today to take better care of you?

- When do you create space and time for quiet contemplation?

DWAIN DEVILLE

*"I'd rather be riding my motorcycle thinking about business
than sitting in an office thinking about my motorcycle."*
- Dwain DeVille

Dwain DeVille worked in the world of banking for fifteen years
before venturing into entrepreneurship with the help of his coach
and many extraordinary mentors. He has published a book called
The Biker's Guide to Business, in which he incorporates his passion
for motorcycles with business principles. He now considers himself
a "Business Navigator."

Dwain teaches CEOs to understand that business is the economic
engine that can take you where you want to go in life, while
reminding them that business itself is not life. He feels that as long
as you're on the right path for the right reasons, and as long as
you're residing in your "sweet spot," no matter how difficult things
get, the right person at the right time will cross your path.

What inspired you to become an entrepreneur?

In the early 1990s I was just coming out of a divorce and met a
lady who was ten years my senior. To this day, she is still the most
impactful person to ever touch my world. A classic entrepreneur,
she started two successful companies. When I met her, she was in
the process of getting out of her second company. She embraced
me and brought me into the world of entrepreneurship. As an
entrepreneur, she hung out with entrepreneurs, and the more I
was around them, the more I felt at home. I started looking at
my existence in the 9-to-5 world and thought, "I have got to get
out of this."

My friend and mentor served as my bridge, patting me on the
back when I needed it – and more importantly, kicking me in the
butt when I needed setting straight. She did something very, very
important as well: she walked away when she was supposed to and

did not remain an artificial crutch. That was an incredible time in my life.

On a daily basis, I'm inspired by the entrepreneurs I work with and hang out with. They may not be the biggest names in the game, or have the most notoriety, but they wake up every day and do it right, because that's who they are and what they're all about. Sometimes I sit back in awe of their integrity, and say, "Yeah, that's why they've been in business for thirty years." While they are making money, they don't just do it for the money.

As an entrepreneur, it's important to look at the environment I've created and make sure it inspires me on a daily basis. Not a day goes by that I don't sit down with someone and have a conversation from which I walk away saying, "Hmm, that was interesting!"

How have you created your life on your terms?

It goes back to something that took place five years ago, when, at the age of forty-eight, I lost my left kidney to cancer. For the next two years, my business continued to go well, and I was happy with that, but I was starting to get restless.

One of the things that I do, some people call coaching. I call it "navigating." I navigate for companies for a living: I take them where they want to go. One day, I was with my coach, and we were talking about how I could live my life with total passion, every day. I realized that to do that, I needed to incorporate my love of motorcycling, which I've done since the age of sixteen, into my business life. My coach looked at me and said, "Well, you do a workshop for entrepreneurs at the local university. Why don't you take it on the road? Do a workshop on wheels for entrepreneurs that like motorcycles?" I sat back and said, "That's brilliant! I'll call it *The Biker's Guide to Business*!"

I got home that night and searched "The Biker's Guide to Business" on Amazon.com. No one had written a book by that title, so I pulled up GoDaddy.com and bought the URL immediately.

Then, I started thinking about how to promote this "workshop on wheels." What I quickly recognized was no one outside my business circles knew me, and that the best way for people to get to know me was to write a book. That's when I started looking at getting into the world of publishing.

Not long after, I was in California, and a friend hooked me up with Mark Victor Hanson's book agent. I had just fifteen minutes to pitch my idea to her. She looked at my twelve-page down-and-dirty proposal, and said, "What do motorcycles and business have in common?"

"Well, recent studies show that every year, 300,000 senior executives making over six figures buy motorcycles," I replied.

"You know, our governor rides a motorcycle," she said thoughtfully. "This is kind of interesting; I'll have to think about it."

A few minutes later I got an e-mail from her saying that she'd discussed my proposal with her team, and that she would love to represent me. I signed with her agency, and shortly thereafter, Wiley and Sons bought my book.

What have you learned from mentors and role models in your life?

I come from a small town in Louisiana, and if I had followed the family path, I would be a school bus driver today. My grandfather had the fifth school bus in our area, and my dad followed in his footsteps. I blew that off.

I've had many, many mentors in my life. The first was the woman who helped me become an entrepreneur. The second is a dear friend of mine who, like my first mentor, is a classic entrepreneur who started two very successful businesses. He and I are motorcycle buddies, and every step of the way I was able to bounce ideas off him. He takes my radical dreams and visions and applies his business sensibility to them. Then, we meet somewhere in the middle and I start to see the next steps laid out for me. He's been there every step of the way, and I would not be where I am today if it weren't for him.

My third mentor is my coach, who unfortunately, had to move away about a year ago. People who look at coaching as frivolous or unnecessary don't know what they're missing. It's incredibly helpful to have someone in your world who doesn't have a dog in your fight, who's just sitting there on the sidelines with you, listening; someone who can look at you and say, "Why the hell are you going there?" or, "When are you going to get this done?" or "That's a great idea, but have you thought about..." I had those conversations with her every two weeks, and there's no way I'd be where I am today if she weren't in my world.

Please share one tip for living a full life:

Discovering how to live a full life is really the crux of what I do on a daily basis.

The average age of the company (not the people, but the company) I work with is thirty years. These businesses have been around for a long time; they've all been successful, and they're good at what they do, but for some reason they can't reach the next level. I see these brilliant entrepreneurs sitting there wondering what the problem is, and I look at them and ask one question: "It's five years from today, and everything in your life has gone according to plan. Every obstacle has been overcome, every goal achieved. Now, tell me what your life looks like."

They can't do it. They have no clue. They can tell me what the company is going to look like five years from now, but when I hit them with the life thing, they're not ready for it. At that point, I say, "Until you can tell me where you want to go in life, I cannot help you in your business. Yes, for the past twenty-five years (or more) you've poured your blood, sweat and tears into this thing and given it everything you've got, but at the end of the day your business is just the economic engine that's going to take you where you want to go in life." What's holding them back isn't their business, but the conflict between life and business.

What starts as a minor shift in perspective is really a major breakthrough. Delegating becomes a little easier, and all of a sudden they don't feel guilty about taking off to ride a motorcycle and talk with Dwain for four hours. They don't feel guilty about taking that five-day weekend to do things with their family, or blowing out of the office every Thursday at 3:00 to go coach their son's soccer team. Now they understand that once established, a business is nothing more than an economic engine to propel us towards our dreams.

What would you like your legacy to be?

That I lived until I died, full out and with total passion. That I had passion for everyone around me; my family, my life, my friends, my business. That when I went after the things I wanted, I never half-stepped, but went all the way with a smile on my face.

Dwain's Message:

Your business is nothing more than the economic engine that will propel you toward your dreams. So stop, dream, and put your life first.

MELINDA COHAN

"Be the change you wish to see in the world."

- Gandhi

Melinda Cohan made an internal commitment to do things her way, instead of playing by other people's rules. The canvas of her life was wiped clean, and she was ready for a new chapter.

She credits her success as an entrepreneur to having the courage to know herself as a woman and a leader at a deep and intimate level, and infuses those powerful feminine qualities and virtues into her business. To her, personal development and starting your own business are inextricably connected; she believes that the decision to strike out on your own can be just as much about healing as it is about creating a rewarding business with a healthy bottom line.

What inspired you to become an entrepreneur?

What started me on the path was an internal decision; the decision to live life on my terms. How do I want my life to be? What do I desire? What are the things I don't really care for? I committed to doing whatever it took – not just from a "working hard" standpoint, but from a deep knowledge that no matter how scary or how overwhelming the process became, I could do it. That decision was the paramount step.

The path of the entrepreneur unfolded from there. I discovered I had the desire and ability to support others in their life accomplishments, and could do so successfully through my own business. I had the help of a lot of mentors and coaches, who helped me learn a new perspective, a new language, and new approaches I was not even aware of. These torch-carriers have been by my side the entire way, even if I've never met them in person.

If you don't want to do a lot of self-improvement, do not start your own business. Your business isn't just created for the sake of what it does or provides; it can also help you work through your own life challenges, and heal many aspects of yourself that may not otherwise have been healed.

How have you created your life on your terms?

Just this morning, a colleague e-mailed me to ask for insider tips and books that might give her insight into how I'm experiencing what I'm experiencing. She said, "You don't observe too many people in everyday life that make you step back and say, 'How can I experience that?'"

It was neat to be reminded that the life I am living is the exact life I created. It's interesting, because that was not my intention – I was going along, "business as usual," just like most of the people in this world. But the universe had different plans for me, and began to get my attention in some very different ways. My life as I knew it crumbled right in front of my face, and I was given the opportunity to rebuild my life on my terms. Some amazing people – coaches, other business owners, authors – came into my life, and presented me with new information and a new perspective that helped me create the life of my dreams. In the last two years, I have accomplished more by doing more of what I love, and I'm celebrating that.

What have you learned from mentors and role models in your life?

Here are some things I've learned (in no particular order) which have deeply impacted my life, and which I infuse into my life every day.

- Live by *The Four Agreements* by Don Miguel Ruiz: Don't Make Assumptions; Be Impeccable With Your Word; Don't Take Things Personally; Always Do Your Best.

- Stay connected to your heart. One of the coaches that I worked with at one time, Dr. Lise Janelle, taught me to always stay connected to my heart, and that the more I live and lead from that place, the more I will continue to create happiness and joy.

- When I discover, acknowledge, and express my own feminine divinity, life becomes one fantastic experience. When we live as Sister Goddesses (Sister because all women are connected; Goddess because we all have a piece of the divine within us), we connect to inherent feminine virtues and characteristics that lead the world through inspiration, collaboration, and pleasure.

- Marketing is a simple and fun conversation of the heart that inspires others.

- From Kate Steinbacher, my business partner, I learned that if fun is not involved, it's not worth doing.

- From my husband, Dave Cohan, I learned the value of finding the holes – the things that aren't working – in a given situation, so that you can plug them quickly and create a situation that will be successful.

- Always apply the Four Rules of Money as taught by Barbara Stanny: Spend Less; Save More; Invest Wisely and Give Generously. In that order.

- To be successful entrepreneurs, we must treat our passions as businesses, and not just hobbies.

- Systems are the key to freedom in business. When we create systems that bring simplicity, consistency and automation to the day-to-day activities of our businesses, we create more time, save energy, and are able to put our attention on the work we love to do.

- Connection to a Higher Power (whether you call it God, Universe, GPS, Buddha, etc.) connects us to the greatest aspect of ourselves, and connects us all to one another. This connection is what brings the sparkle to our lives.

- As we allow our lights to shine, we unconsciously give others permission to do the same.

Please share one tip for living a full life:

I host Extraordinary Women Gatherings to support women in living extraordinary lives. One thing I would say to women entrepreneurs out there is to come from your feminine essence.

Live and lead from the Goddess. Know the divine feminine within you. Tap into that energy: embrace it, accept it, love it, honor it, and it will grow. As a result, you cannot help but experience the life of your dreams.

What would you like your legacy to be?

I'd like to be the model and example for how women entrepreneurs – whether they are stay-at-home entrepreneurs leading their families or the CEOs of corporations – can turn their passions into thriving businesses led from the heart and spirit by infusing them with their feminine power.

Melinda's Message:

Nurture and honor your own divine energy. Discover how your business creates opportunities for self-study. Integrate lessons from your coaches, friends, and mentors into your everyday existence.

TONY HSIEH

"Don't let your character change color with your environment. Find out who you are and let it stay its true color."
- Rachel Scott

Tony Hsieh has been an entrepreneur all his life. He started his first mail-order business in middle school, and later, created a pizza business to serve his college dormitory.

According to Tony, the worst-case scenario is never that bad. This enlightened attitude allowed him to step up and invest in Zappos. com. He believes in regular personal introspection, and says it's important to take a step back from the day-to-day routine to be certain you're still happy with what you're doing.

What inspired you to become an entrepreneur?

I've been fairly entrepreneurial all my life. In middle school, I ran a mail-order business. While at Harvard, I ran the Quincy House Grille and decided to expand the food selection there by investing in pizza ovens. I ran a pizza business in college with my roommate on the ground floor of our dorm and served 300-400 people.

How have you created your life on your terms?

I think it's just realizing that the worst-case scenario is really not that bad. We live in a society where no matter what happens, it's unlikely that we will have to worry about actually starving to death. I realized that in the worst-case scenario, there are always friends that you can stay with, or even strangers you can stay with through sites such as couchsurfing.com.

What have you learned from mentors and role models in your life?

I have found most of my mentors through books. You can see a list of a lot of the books I've read at www.zappos.com/zappos-library. Many of our customers and partners ask us, "What inspires the Zappos culture and the mantra POWERED by SERVICE?" One way we can share that with our community is the Zappos Library: here, you'll find a collection of books that get us fired up about our customers, the products we buy, and the world we live in.

Please share one tip for living a full life:

I think it's important to take a step back from the business of the day-to-day every once in a while (or even once a week) and ask yourself why you're doing what you're doing, and if it's truly making you happy. Be really honest with yourself when answering.

What would you like your legacy to be?

I'm not really trying to create a legacy. I'm just trying to impact the world in a positive way.

Tony's Message:

Free yourself from limitations by understanding that the worst-case scenario is never that bad.

JULIE SWATEK

"Leap, and the net will appear."
- John Burroughs

Julie Swatek is a fourth-generation entrepreneur, and feels that entrepreneurship chose her. She discovered the scrapbooking business, and her passion, at age thirty-five.

Julie thrives on her connections with other women, and works to help them realize that they are not alone in their feelings. She created a life on her own terms by choosing to put all of her energy toward success.

What inspired you to become an entrepreneur?

It's funny: I don't think you choose to become an entrepreneur. I think it chooses you. I happen to be a fourth-generation entrepreneur. I think it also has to do with the way you grow up: when you're an entrepreneur, you look at things differently than other people.

When I was growing up, it was normal for my parents to say they were going to start another business; it was something that happened regularly through my childhood years. It took me a while to get to that entrepreneurial state of my life. Having grown up with entrepreneurs, I knew that your business is something you have to love from the bottom of your toes, and understand that you are going to commit your life to. I worked in the accounting industry for a long time, and always knew I was going to have my own business one day – I just didn't know when it would happen. I hadn't found anything I was so passionate enough about that I could live and breathe it every single day.

When my daughter was an infant, I took her with me to find plaster so I could make a plaster cast of her hand for my husband's first Father's Day. I walked into a scrapbook store for the first time in my life. It was one of those times when you realize there is an entirely different world out there that you don't know anything about. I was like, "Wow!" There were rows and rows of albums, stickers, and pretty papers, and I had this brand new life that I was trying to document.

The number one reason why women start scrapbooking is the birth of a child. Before you have a child, you're on your own in life; it's kind of just about you. When I had my first child, I became aware that I'm just one link in a chain that extended way before me and is going to extend way beyond me.

I instantly became obsessed with scrapbooking.

It took a couple of years, though, to realize I could actually make a business out of it. When I was thirty-five years old and five months pregnant with my son, I found out that the job I had been working at for almost six years was going through a corporate merger, and that I would be laid off, along with ninety-seven other people. The last scheduled day of my employment was the day my son was due to be born. Jobs for pregnant women are not exactly falling off trees, so I decided my business would be Plan B – something I could start slowly, so maybe someday it would take off. I threw myself into it. I was very fortunate that my husband's income was enough to support our family, so there was no pressure on me. I was able to take every dime I made and put it into the scrapbooking business.

Fast forward seven years, to today. We almost broke the three million mark this year. We have a 7,000-square-foot warehouse and twenty employees. Not a day goes by that I don't walk around and say to myself, "Oh my gosh! All these people are here because of me!"

How have you created your life on your terms?

I walked away from my thirteen-year marriage this year. My friend's husband was killed in a car accident recently, and I realized that if life could change in an instant, this couldn't be my life. This couldn't be as good as it ever got. I filed for divorce, and moved out of the house we built and into my own condo. I am starting over on a multitude of levels, but I am the happiest I've been in a very long time, and I am grateful that I started my own business seven years ago. So often, divorce is a major financial setback for women. I am incredibly fortunate not to be in that situation.

But starting that business? Scary is the first word that comes to mind. Exhilarating, too. Looking back on it now, it was scary because I didn't know anything! I started a web site knowing nothing about the process. I'm not an incredibly artistic person, and I had no idea what I wanted for a layout. What I did have going for me is that I'd spent my entire career in business; I think that's one of the reasons I've been so successful. I understood cash flow, management and profits. Three years into the business, though, I still didn't know what keywords were, and I didn't understand search engine optimization. I remember moving into my first commercial space, and thinking the phones were just like the ones at home! I had no idea the effort that went into the technical side of things. I look back on the woman I was then, and think, "You poor thing! You didn't know anything!" But I did know that I would do whatever I had to in order to be successful. Whatever resource, book, or mentor I had to find, I was going to do it. And I did.

What have you learned from mentors and role models in your life?

I was the first recipient of the Athena Power Link mentorship in the state of Florida. That changed everything. One day I called Tom Kruczek, the head of my advisory panel (he was the Director for the Center for Entrepreneurship at Rollins College, he's now doing the same thing at Syracuse), and I said, "I don't know what to do." He basically said, "Just lean back on us. We're here. We will hold you up and believe in you, even if you don't believe in yourself right now."

That statement summed up my entire experience. As financially savvy as I thought I was, it was a shock when a banker walked in and told me I was going out of business. We had grown 652% the year before I got the mentorship program, but the banker said, "You'll be out of money in six months. You're growing too fast." I knew that was the reason I applied for the mentorship: I knew that I could successfully grow myself out of business.

One rule for the Athena program is that you can't do business with anyone that sits on your panel. The banker stepped down from my panel so she could loan me money, because the big bank I was dealing with wouldn't loan me anything. I would have gone out of business if wasn't for this great woman. I've had help from insurance people; my CPA, who still two years later I consider a friend; and Dwain DeVille, my mentor with a capital "M." Dwain will ask me questions that just infuriate me, but he's always totally on my side.

Please share one tip for living a full life:

"Selfish" isn't a bad word. If you are like a bucket that has a big hole in the bottom, there's no way you can ever fill yourself up. You have to take responsibility for your own life. That doesn't mean that there's no room in your life for anybody else.

What would you like your legacy to be?

As a parent, you always hope that your children don't go through the same struggles that you did – but those struggles are what turned you into the person you are now. I don't wish that my children don't struggle; I just wish that they have different, better struggles, and that they can learn from watching me. Whether that means they are fifth-generation entrepreneurs or not, I hope I can pass on some of my strengths to them. (My money is on my daughter, who seems to have inherited the entrepreneur gene from me.)

My legacy? To make the world a little bit better each day. I am so fortunate to connect with over 60,000 people through my weekly e-mail and my blog. I live my life out loud so everyone can learn from my mistakes. I have been given the incredible gift of helping people preserve their memories in a way that is meaningful to them. They have given me their permission to share my thoughts with them, and I have given my permission to them to share back.

At the end of the day, we're all just trying to get through life as best we can. We all share the same struggles and triumphs. It's nice to know there is someone out there who feels just like you do.

Julie's Message:

Creating a life on your terms isn't just about building a business: it's about realizing that life is too short to settle. Take responsibility for your life, and throw yourself unreservedly into your passion.

AFTERWORD

The Common Thread

"We must let go of the life we have planned,
so as to accept the life that is waiting for us."
- Joseph Campbell

To boldly go where no one else has gone before is a sexy idea. Sexier still is discovering mentors, explorers and visionaries who are willing to share the bold steps they have already taken along with the lessons they learned along the way. Often times all we ever have to do is explore our curiosity.

I wanted to learn the secrets of living the entrepreneurial dream, so I began inviting intriguing entrepreneurs to be a part of this book. Why? Because I am a delightfully curious woman! At the start of this project, I couldn't have imagined the scope and breadth of the result.

The stories included in this book introduced you to a group of people who summoned the courage to make an extraordinary life for themselves on their own terms. Every interview is a gift, and can help you add a few details to your personal roadmap to success. Follow your own curiosity; you never know where it will lead you!

Despite their incredibly different lives, there are common threads among all of the interviewees in this book which collectively constitute the keys to living your dreams: passion, awareness, support, trust, destiny, and courage. Each individual knew they were meant for something more than performing an unrewarding job and collecting a paycheck. I found it incredibly interesting that not one of these entrepreneurs mentioned money or material things as a primary goal. To them, success is defined in broader, more ephemeral terms.

Out of all the "keys" we've discovered here, passion is probably the most important. If you were locked in a windowless room, passion would be the key that opens the door. When you are in the presence of a passionate person, the world falls away, and you are suddenly swept up in a tidal wave of possibility. The world is a playground for people who have the courage to follow their bliss.

In the span of these interviews, the passionate drive to create a joyful life is described more than anything else. Whether it was sparked by an idea, devotion to family, or the burning desire to change a circumstance, everyone in these pages is filled with passion.

Awareness is another thread that connects each visionary in these pages. Awareness allows you to look for opportunities in your surroundings, but also to understand how your mind perceives opportunity. Most of the entrepreneurs I interviewed were bold and direct in their awareness, standing before the Universe as if to say, "This is it! I am ready to make a difference, and I will fulfill my dreams."

Passion combined with awareness leads to opportunity, and the courage to take action with passion must be nourished from loving support. Everyone mentioned having a strong support system of friends, family, or mentors in place. The strong underlying message is that you are who you surround yourself with. If you're feeling unsupported in your endeavors, look around: are you surrounded by people who are full of fire and light, or people who live in negativity and darkness?

In order to take the significant risk of changing your life, you need to have trust – not only in your support system, but in something deeper as well. All of the interviewees in this book mentioned trust, whether it was in God, the Universe, a Higher Power, their gut, or their intuition. While having faith was not always an easy proposition, they understood that without confidence and trust they would remain stuck.

Sometimes, a major change is prompted by a feeling that you're destined for something greater. Especially if you're aware of your passion, you're probably sure that your destiny does not involve slaving for a paycheck in an office, or feeding into the psychotic loop of drama and office politics. All of the interviewees had a strong desire to create a business that complemented their own natural rhythms. Some have even gone so far as to consciously create their own "company culture" in order to solidify their values and make sure that selfless giving, teamwork, and positive thinking are always the first priority.

Most interesting of all (at least to me) is that many of the people I interviewed said that entrepreneurship "happened" to them: they did not choose it. "I just knew I had to do this," is a common theme. Each had the courage to act on their instincts, while understanding their personal responsibility for creating their dreams. Many had the moxie to explore several ideas before finding the perfect fit. These individuals have paved my way, and yours, toward liberation, and Life on Your Own Terms.

Yours in Liberation,

ABOUT THE AUTHOR

Shann Vander Leek

"To be nobody but yourself – in a world which is doing its best, night and day, to make you like everybody else – means to fight the hardest battle which any human being can fight – and never stop fighting."

-E.E. Cummings

After eighteen years of serving the television broadcast model of Corporate America, and over a decade of leading a talented sales force responsible for millions of dollars in revenue, Shann Vander Leek reinvented herself as the founder of True Balance Life Coaching and Cofounder of Seize True Success Coaching. She is a Coach Training Alliance Certified Coach and Certified Yoga Instructor with a Bachelors degree from Western Michigan University in Communications and Marketing.

Shann is the best-selling coauthor of a series of team-authored books for women titled, *Wake Up Women: Be Happy, Healthy & Wealthy*, and the author of *Getting Your Groove Back: A Guide to Luscious Living*. She is the co-creator of AnxietySlayer.com, a web resource dedicated to helping people achieve peace and tranquility through anxiety release exercises and supportive tools.

Shann's background in broadcast television advertising sales, marketing, and client development, along with her experience as a sales force leader, prepared her for the business of professional coaching. Her personal style and direct approach have assisted hundreds of people in overcoming personal and professional challenges. Telephone and e-mail consultations make her accessible to clients all over the world.

Contact Shann to schedule a Life on Your Terms Accelerator session today!

Shann Vander Leek, CTA-CC, CYT, RYT
Life on Your Terms Accelerator™
Telephone: (231) 668-9850
Skype: Shannolann
Blog: www.lifeonyourtermsbook.net
Web site: www.truebalancelifecoaching.com
Twitter: @ShannVanderLeek
Facebook: www.facebook.com/shannvanderleek

243

LIFE ON YOUR TERMS ACCELERATOR™ COACHING TOOLS

The Life on Your Terms Accelerator™ series includes workbooks, CDs and downloadable content to support you through your next significant transition.

Visit www.lifeonyourtermsbook.net to learn more about this supportive and powerful coaching series.

Written specifically to help you follow your passion and create your life on your terms, this body of work reflects a lifetime of experience and provides the support you need to gracefully transition to the path of your dreams.

The Life on Your Terms Accelerator™ series contains practical information and simple steps to move you forward through your next transition. Each workbook is designed to:

- Help you clarify your life's purpose and passion.
- Help you understand the stages of transition.
- Create a future aligned with who you are.
- Overcome issues around the illusion of job security.
- Remove issues or obstacles including fear and doubt.
- Offer tools, resources and practices to help you succeed faster.

Are you interested in sharing your personal liberation story? We'd love to learn more about your path to entrepreneurial freedom! We will be featuring a new liberation story each month on the Life on Your Terms Blog. You can find us at:

Blog: Life on Your Terms – www.lifeonyourtermsbook.net
Facebook: Life on Your Terms – www.facebook.com/lifeonyourterms
Twitter: @LifeAccelerator

ENTREPRENEUR CONTACT INFORMATION

Askew, Nic

Nic is many things: filmmaker, storyteller, poet, musician, composer, and commentator on our experience of life. In his most recent film series, *Soul Biographies*, he captures the experience of being human, and offers viewers the opportunity to be moved to tears, laughter, and a deeper experience of themselves.

Title: Founder of Soul Biographies
Telephone: (612) 326-6882
Web site: www.soulbiographies.com
E-mail: nic@soulbiographies.com

Babauta, Leo

Leo is the creator and writer of Zen Habits, a blog dedicated to simple productivity. He lives in Guam with his wife and six children. He also created mnmlist.com (on minimalism) and Write To Done (for writers and bloggers). He is the author of a best-selling book, *The Power of Less: The Fine Art of Limiting Yourself to the Essential, in Business and in Life.*

Title: Author and Creator
Web site: www.zenhabits.net
E-mail: leo.babauta@gmail.com

Battishill, Arlene

Don't ever tell Arlene something isn't possible: she will take that as her cue to insist that it is, and set about proving it! Arlene is determined to live on her own terms and spends a lot of time encouraging other people to do the same. She sees people trapped in their lives and tries to show, through example, that anything is possible. She hopes that her own story will be an inspiration for others to reach for whatever it is that inspires them. You only get to live each day once, so go and be fabulous!

Title: President & CEO, Scooter Girls, Inc.
Telephone: (323) 203-7411
Web site: www.scooter-girls.com
E-mail: arlene@scooter-girls.com

Bedsow Horgan, Susie

During her many life experiences, Susie discovered that one of her greatest strengths and deepest desires was to be of service to people. Following that trail, she enrolled in the training program for co-active coaching offered by The Coaches Training Institute. As a result of this journey, she developed her niche: "Designing the next act of your life."

Title: Susie Bedsow Horgan, CPCC, Personal Life Coach
Telephone: (203) 834-2869
Web site: www.getalifewithsusie.com
E-mail: susie@getalifewithsusie.com

Blaha, Jim

After twenty-five years of climbing the corporate ladder at Westinghouse, Jim woke up one day and asked himself the question, "Who am I, and what do I want to do with the rest of my life?" With a wife to support and three boys in college, he answered his own question, and made the change that led him to become an investment banker and business valuation expert with an entrepreneurial state of mind.

Title: Principal at BHC/JJB
Web site: www.linkedin.com/pub/jim-blaha/4/6a6/b9b
E-mail: jjbgeneva@aol.com

Boyd, Arleen

Arleen Boyd understands that we each must take responsibility for the condition of our personal economy, and recognizes that individuals and companies must come together to excel. "Aloha Arleen" podcasts feature education, experiences, and interviews with experts in the different aspects of online marketing, and help businesses apply marketing strategies.

Title: Aloha Arleen
Web site: www.alohaarleen.com
E-mail: arleen@alohaarleen.com

Castillo Holley, Alicia

Alicia Castillo Holley is an expert in creating wealth. She is passionate about entrepreneurship, innovation and venture capital. Her views about prosperity inspire and motivate individuals to be actors rather than spectators in their own lives. She worked as a scientist and professor before becoming involved in product development, and eventually turning into an entrepreneur and angel investor.

Title: CEO, Wealthing Group®
Telephone: 0400217020
Web site: www.wealthing.com
E-mail: aliciacastillo@wealthing.com

Clynes, Tom

Tom Clynes is a freelance journalist and photographer who covers environmental issues, science, and adventure travel. As a contributing editor for *National Geographic Adventure* and *Popular Science*, he has reported on Ebola outbreaks and eco-mercenaries in central Africa, retraced Edmund Hillary's climbs in New Zealand, and learned to fly in the Australian outback. He is also the author of the book *Wild Planet*.

Title: Freelance Journalist and Photographer
Web site: www.tomclynes.com
E-mail: tomclynes@mindspring.com

Cohan, Melinda

Melinda Cohan is a woman of vision who believes that spirit and business go hand in hand – or as she would say, heart in heart. As Visionary, President, and cofounder of The Coaches Console™ Melinda combines spirit and business in a unique manner that allows her to share her knowledge with other coaches as the coaching industry as a whole.

Title: Cofounder and CEO of The Coaches Console®
Telephone: (540) 314-9779
Web site: www.coachesconsole.com
E-mail: melinda@coachesconsole.com

Cohen, Lorraine

As a spiritual minister, life coach, hypnotherapist, counselor, published writer, inspirational speaker, and radio broadcaster, Lorraine's great joy is helping people awaken to who they are, who they are meant to be, and what they here to do. For more than twenty years, she has helped thousands of spiritually-minded business owners, entrepreneurs, coaches, professionals, and leaders from a wide range of industries create prosperous businesses, meaningful careers, and fulfilling lives aligned with Spirit.

Title: CEO and Founder of Powerful Living
Telephone: (610) 415-1733
Web site: www.powerfull-living.biz
E-mail: lorraine@powerfull-living.biz

Crow, Lynette

Lynette has played an integral role in many start-up companies' multi-product market expansion. For more than a decade, she has been responsible for corporate infrastructure which she designed to support excellence in client management and clinic operations. Her natural problem-solving ability has played a key role in companies' productivity, and her vision has allowed them to achieve unprecedented growth and expansion.

Title: President/CEO, Conspire2Hire
Telephone: (719) 785-1161
Web site: www.conspire2hire.com
E-mail: lcrow@conspire2hire.com

DeVille, Dwain

Dwain M. DeVille is the author of *The Biker's Guide to Business*, and CEO of WaterMark International, Inc., a consultancy that serves entrepreneurial business leaders. As much as Dwain loves the challenges of business, he loves to ride his motorcycle even more, and after decades of enjoying both, he's equally at home in the boardroom and in the saddle. He now spends his time helping entrepreneurs regain balance between their business and personal lives.

Title: Author of *The Bikers Guide to Business* and CEO, WaterMark International
Web site: www.dwaindeville.com and www.bikersguidetobusiness.com
E-mail: navigator@bikersguidetobusiness.com

Edey, Lorraine

As a therapist, Lorraine was aware of how her patients struggled with money management and financial decisions. After transitioning into coaching, she saw the same money issues running rampant among her clients. Lorraine's desire was to provide a plan for clients to reach their financial goals; now, as a Money and Relationship Coach, Lorraine offers full support with her "Extreme Money Makeover™."

Title: Founder, Coaching Inspirations
Telephone: (321) 288-0692
Web site: www.coachinginspirations.com
E-mail: loridey@aol.com

Farrell, Ann

As a successful executive, and now as a successful leader and business coach, Ann not only knows how to coach success, she knows how to create it! Using her trademarked tools and programs, Ann supports her clients and their teams and organizations to help them step up into breakthrough results. Her clients include more than twenty Fortune 500 Companies, and over twenty-five licensed Corporate Coaching firms now use Ann's coaching engagement models as their standard for excellence.

Contact Ann to learn more about her company, Quantum Endeavors®, Inc. and her member-based executive coaching program, Your Corporate Success.

Title: Corporate and Business Success Coach
Telephone: (630) 743-1552
Web site: www.quantumendeavors.com
E-mail: ann@quantumendeavors.com

Fields, Jonathan

Jonathan Fields is a writer, entrepreneur, marketing and small-biz strategist, and author of *Career Renegade: How To Make a Great Living Doing What You Love* (Broadway Books, 2009). He has been featured extensively in the media, including *The New York Times, The Wall Street Journal, Business Week, USA Today, People, Fast Company*, NBC, CNBC, CBS Radio, *Entrepreneur, Self, Vogue*, and *Fitness*, plus thousands of web sites. Jonathan speaks regularly on lifestyle, entrepreneurship, marketing, and the book business, and shares his thoughts online at TribalAuthor.com and through his popular blog at JonathanFields.com.

When he's not working, you can find Jonathan dancing around his living room with his wife and daughter; occasionally, he also sleeps.

Title: Entrepreneur
Telephone: (646) DRIVE-08
Web site: www.jonathanfields.com
E-mail: jonathan@jonathanfields.com

Foote, John

John Foote, a twenty-year veteran of the film and entertainment industry, owner of Land Mind Productions, and lifelong punk rocker, founded Mental Records in 1995. John established the label after returning to Southern Oregon from L.A. fueled by a passion to create and direct music videos.

Title: Owner of Land Mind Productions and Mental Records
Web site: www.mentalrecords.net
E-mail: info@mentalfilms.com

Gaines, Akemi

Akemi Gaines has the uncanny ability to read people's soul records (called Akashic Records). While she assists personal development enthusiasts with her reading and coaching, she intends to innovate new spiritual services, so that this industry can gain public recognition and respect. She is the author of the Real Life Spirituality blog, where she shares insights on various aspects of life.

Title: Founder, Akashic Record Reading
Web site: www.akashicrecordreading.com and www.reallifespirituality.com
E-mail: akemi@reallifespirituality.com

Guthmiller, Dava

Dava Guthmiller is the founder & Creative Director of Noise 13 Design, Inc., the founder of Pow.wow Network, and the leader of Slow Food San Francisco. Her background and passion lies in lifestyle branding, including food & beverage, hospitality, beauty and leisure. Being involved in Slow Food, and creating events like the Localize Dinner Series, speaks to her passion for all things good for the environment and for the body.

Title: CEO & Creative Director for Noise 13
Telephone: (415) 957-1313
Web site: www.noise13.com
E-mail: dava@noise13.com

Helbig, Diane

Diane is an internationally recognized author, business and leadership development coach, speaker, and workshop facilitator. As a certified professional Coach, and president of Seize This Day Coaching, Diane helps businesses and organizations operate more constructively and profitably. She is also cofounder of Seize True Success, a coaching practice dedicated to helping franchisees grow and prosper. She offers workshops, speeches, and seminars on the subjects of sales, business development, and leadership. Diane is the author of *Lemonade Stand Selling*, a sales book for small business owners, and is also a contributing author to *Chicken Soup for the Soul: Power Moms*.

Title: Owner of Seize This Day Coaching
Telephone: (216) 534-2030
Web site: www.seizethisdaycoaching.com
E-mail: diane@seizethisdaycoaching.com

Hsieh, Tony

Tony originally got involved with Zappos as an advisor and investor in 1999, two months after the company was founded. He joined Zappos full-time in 2000. Under his leadership, Zappos has increased its gross merchandise sales from $1.6 million in 2000 to over $1 billion in 2008 by focusing relentlessly on customer service. Prior to joining Zappos, Tony cofounded Venture Frogs and LinkExchange.

Title: CEO, Zappos
Web site: www.zappos.com
E-mail: pr@zappos.com

Janes, Aprille

Aprille Janes is a certified Life Coach and a champion of women who long to claim the bigger life they know is waiting! She teaches that the best way for women to reclaim that "Bolder Chick" inside is to connect to their irresistible core of passion, and helps her clients make that connection through her writing classes, workshops and private coaching. Start your journey by downloading her free e-book *Passion, Purpose and Values* from her web site.

Title: Founder of Bolder Woman
Telephone: (905) 985-6454
Web sites: www.aprillejanes.com and www.bolderwoman.com
E-mail: aprille@inbox.com

Joy, Linda

Living her soul's purpose, "conscious entrepreneur" Linda Joy is dedicated to inspiring women to live deeper, more authentic, inspired lives. She is the Publisher of *Aspire* Magazine, the premiere inspirational magazine for women; and the founder of Inspired Living Publishing, publisher of a series of inspirational anthologies for women and by women, including *A Juicy, Joyful Life: Inspiration From Women Who Have Found The Sweetness In Every Day.*

Title: President and Founder, Aspire Media, Inc.
Founder and Publisher, Inspired Living Publishing
Telephone: (508) 265-7929
Web sites: www.aspiremag.net and www.inspiredlivingpublishing.com
E-mail: linda@aspiremag.net

Kanbar, Jeff

Jeff Kanbar is a native New Yorker and entrepreneur with a background in spirits, restaurants, real estate, design, and manufacturing. He got his first taste of the liquor business when his uncle, Maurice Kanbar, started SKYY Vodka out of his San Francisco apartment in 1992. When SKYY was launched in New York City in 1994,

Jeff came on board as the sole sales, marketing, and promotions director. After four years with SKYY, Jeff embarked on various endeavors on his own, but always missed the excitement of the liquor business. "My appetite for traveling the world, experiencing new spirits and nightlife culture only got stronger as I got older." Jeff then decided the time was ripe to go on his own and produce the spirit he had been craving.

Title: Founder of Jett Spirits, LLC
Telephone: (323) 655-JETT (5388)
Web site: www.drinkjett.com
E-mail: jeff@drinkjett.com

Lamphere, Matt

Matt Lamphere is an independent filmmaker & martial artist. His mission is simple: to tell the highest quality visual stories that he can, while continuing to refine his craft. Visit his web site for further information on projects in development and the services his video production company offers.

Title: Owner, Visual Media Tactics and VMT Films
Telephone: (231) 342-4230
Web site: www.visualmediatactics.com and www.vmtfilms.com
E-mail: matt@visualmediatactics.com

Lopez, Laura

Recently featured on *The Today Show*, Laura Lopez has been leading teams and achieving results for major Fortune 100 Companies since the early 1980s. Most recently, Laura was a highly successful Vice President for The Coca-Cola Company. As a speaker, award-winning author, and Birkman certified coach, Laura helps clients build more sustainable personal and professional results to achieve greater levels of success.

Title: Award-winning Author, Motivational Speaker,
and Certified Birkman Method Coach
Telephone: (713) 828-8829
Web site: www.laura-lopez.com
E-mail: laura@laura-lopez.com

MacQuarrie, Joe

Joe MacQuarrie is a world traveler, lover of life, and advertising media specialist. Joe removes the stress and frustration of planning, managing, and implementing advertising plans, and provides a highly professional advertising placement service with more than twenty years experience in sales, marketing and advertising.

Title: Owner, Advertising Advantage
Telephone: (231) 883-3563
Web site: www.adplacementadvantage.com
E-mail: joemacquarrie@me.com

Martin, Deborah

Deborah Martin is a Master Certified Coach, Professional Mentor Coach, writer, outdoor adventurer, fisherwoman, avid canoeist, and lover of nature. Deb is extraordinarily intuitive, and passionate about all things wild. She spends much of her time getting to know herself better and testing her limits in the wilderness, and gives Mother Nature credit for being her first coach. In addition to her regular one-on-one coaching sessions, Deb combines her intuitive abilities and her passion for nature to offer what she calls Wilderness Adventure Coaching.

Title: Owner of Portage Coach
Telephone: (231) 879-4178
Web site: www.portagecoach.com
E-mail: deb@portagecoach.com

Merkel, Anne

Dr. Anne Merkel is The Corporate Alchemist, and takes her title from the energetic shifts she has facilitated in individuals, projects, teams, and organizations worldwide over the last thirty years. Like an Alchemist of old, changing lead into gold, Anne inspires, energizes, and transforms individual and corporate clients. Wherever she goes, conscious transformation follows. Anne is a leader, coach, change agent, intuitive, Reiki master, energy therapist, and writer who has successfully guided individuals, projects, teams, and organizations from all over the U.S. and Canada, and over seventy-six countries.

Title: The Corporate Alchemist
Telephone: (706) 374-6460 / Toll Free: 1 (877) 262-2276
Web site: www.arielagroup.com
E-mail: merakel@arielagroup.com

Michalowicz, Michael

Mike Michalowicz (pronounced mi-CAL-o-witz) started his first business at the age of twenty-four, after moving his young family to the only safe place he could afford – a retirement village. With limited resources and no experience, he systematically bootstrapped a multi-million dollar technology business, sleeping in conference rooms to avoid hotel costs. After selling his first company, Mike launched a new business the very next day, and in less than three years, sold it to a Fortune 500. With his newest multi-million dollar venture, Obsidian Launch, he fosters startup businesses with his "get rich right" approach. He is author of the wildly popular book for entrepreneurs, *The Toilet Paper Entrepreneur.*

Title: Founder of Obsidian Launch and Author of *The Toilet Paper Entrepreneur*
Telephone: (973) 453-4534 x201
Web site: www.toiletpaperentrepreneur.com
E-mail: mikem@obsidianlaunch.com

Niehaus, Perry

Perry Niehaus is the president and owner of Laser Valley Technologies Corporation. Perry enjoys the study of human psychology, spirituality, motivation, leadership, and personal and group achievement. He loves to play golf, and embraces life coaching and mentorship. Perry dreams of one day providing public service through speaking, teaching, and writing.

Title: General Manager, Laser Valley Technologies Corp.
Telephone: (604) 888-7085
Web site: www.laservalley.com
E-mail: pmniehaus@laservalley.com

Rigsby-Kunz, Bea

Bea Rigsby-Kunz is a retired classroom educator who has taken her new career as an educator in the fields literally. She is the owner of Sage Hill Farms, a sustainable farm project. Both Sage Hill and Bea are works in progress.

Title: Owner, Sage Hill Farms
Telephone: (931) 438-8328
Web site: www.sagehillfarmsandvintagestore.com
E-mail: beakunz@bellsouth.net

Shebani, Ilham

Ilham Shebani supports and motivates women in business to network, collaborate, and create greater opportunities through mentoring partnerships, social media, and local networking events. She creates a platform for women to engage in local and cross-border projects such as International Women's Day, International Fashion Shows, multicultural festivals, interfaith initiatives, and community based events in the UK and MENA region.

Title: Founder and Project Leader of BUILD SELF GROUP
Telephone: 971-50-108-1217 (UAE) 44-79642839-47 (UK)
Web site: www.buildselfgroup.com
E-mail: buildselfgroup@yahoo.co.uk

Slattery, Felicia J.

Felicia J. Slattery lives her life with energy, passion and enthusiasm because she realizes each moment is precious. After nearly losing her life in childbirth in 2004, she began to put her communication and public speaking talents to use to create a positive impact on the world through teaching, writing, consulting and coaching. With two Master's Degrees – one in Adult Education and Training and another in Communication – Felicia specializes in training busy professionals to succeed through effective communication and by delivering results-driven presentations. Her enthusiastic passion for communication is contagious because she knows that one important message delivered with power can transform a life.

Title: Felicia J. Slattery, M.A., M.Ad.Ed.,
Communication Consultant, Speaker and Coach
Telephone: (630) 554-0636
Web site: www.communicationtransformation.com
E-mail: felicia@communicationtransformation.com

Stratten, Scott

Scott Stratten is the President of UnMarketing, a company that helps companies stop marketing and start engaging with their customers. As a leader in the fields of viral marketing, social media, and customer relations, he's taught clients how to create lifelong fans instead of one-off customers. He's been mentioned in publications like *Fast Company*, *The Wall Street Journal*, and *USA Today*, to name a few. That plus $5 gets him a free cup of coffee wherever he goes. His book *UnMarketing: Stop Marketing. Start Engaging* is due to be released in September 2010 by Wiley & Sons.

Title: President of UnMarketing
Telephone: (888) 580-9969
Web site: www.un-marketing.com
Twitter: @UnMarketing

Strelecky, John P.

John P. Strelecky is the #1 Bestselling inspirational author of *The Why Cafe*, *Life Safari*, *The Big Five for Life: Leadership's Greatest Secret*, and *How to be Rich and Happy*. His works have been translated into nineteen languages. John was honored alongside Oprah Winfrey, Tony Robbins, Wayne Dyer, and Deepak Chopra as one of the 100 Most Influential Thought Leaders in the field of leadership and personal development. He has been invited to speak alongside Nobel Peace Prize nominees and award winning philanthropists to share his learning with audiences around the world.

Title: Inspirational Author/Speaker
Web site: www.bigfiveforlife.com
E-mail: jstrelecky@bigfiveforlife.com

Swatek, Julie

Julie Swatek is the founder of www.ScrapYourTrip.com, the most popular e-commerce web site specializing in travel and theme-specific scrapbook supplies. She founded the company in 2002 out of the spare bedroom of her house and has guided it to almost $3 million in revenue. She is a fourth-generation entrepreneur and single mom to two elementary school children. She is governed by the philosophy that when you take care of your employees and customers, the profits will take care of themselves.

Title: Founder, ScrapYourTrip.com
Telephone: (407) 351-1501
Web site: www.scrapyourtrip.com
E-mail: julie@scrapyourtrip.com

Tamaki, Stacie

Whether she's teaching brides and grooms how to plan fun and flirty weddings, advocating for shelter dogs or the National Marrow Donor Program, or just kicking back and eating a cupcake, Stacie lives each moment to its fullest, and always has fun doing it. She's discovered that the key to happiness in life and business is a simple formula: Be kind, be patient, ask for and embrace constructive criticism, embrace change, and always be willing to take chances.

Title: Founder of The Flirty Guide
Telephone: (408) 338-9970
Web site: www.theflirtyguide.com
E-mail: stacie@stacietamaki.com

Vinton, Lisa

Lisa Vinton is President/CEO and founder of Services for Success, Inc., a Southern California business management consulting firm, and cohost of Only 2 Degrees, which has fun connecting people from all over the world to promote business. Her latest book, *How to Get Poor Quick: 10 Myths That Can Cause Your Business to Fail*, is a practical confidence builder for displaced workers in this deep economic recession.

Title: President/CEO, Services For Success
Telephone: (951) 304-0488
Web site: www.services4success.com
E-mail: lisa@services4success.com

Weidlein, Marianne

Marianne is a facilitator, mentor, and author, with expertise in self-mastery, peak performance, relationship, intentional manifestation, and self-employment. She brings 40+ years of experience in business, human potential development, and awakening spiritual awareness to help people achieve peace, success, and freedom on all levels. Her books are *Empowering Vision for Dreamers, Visionaries & Other Entrepreneurs*, and *The Passage to Freedom* (due out in 2010).

Title: Author, Coach and Visionary
Telephone: (303) 903-6366
Web site: www.empoweringvision.com
E-mail: mweidlein@empoweringvision.com

Wilkinson, Will

Will Wilkinson has earned a living with his imagination since childhood. A television entertainer, interview host, author, life coach, designer, and workshop presenter, Will empowers all who know him to become "imagineers," to create the life they want, heal wounds, and provide themselves with the most timely personal growth.

Title: Founder and CIO of Imagifi Productions Unlimited
Telephone: (541) 552-0877
Web site: www.imagifi.com
E-mail: willw@imagifi.com

Zichermann, Gabe

Gabe Zichermann developed the concept for rmbrME after realizing that tracking and connecting with new contacts had become unmanageable. Rather than starting a 12-step program for social hunters, Gabe helped develop rmbrME, the first mobile solution for exchanging social contact and lead information that works with any device. Now residing in New York City, Gabe frequently muses about the opportunities to use game design in broader applications on his blog, www.funwareblog.com. He is the coauthor of the upcoming book, *WebPlay* (Manning, 2009).

Title: CEO and Cofounder, rmbrME
Telephone: (646) 416-6630
Web site: www.rmbrme.com
E-mail: gabe@rmbr.com

References

Ruiz, Miguel, Janet Mills, and Miguel Ruiz. 2000. *The Four Agreements Companion Book: Using The Four Agreements To Master The Dream Of Your Life*. San Rafael, Calif: Amber-Allen Pub.

Levoy, Gregg. 1997. *Callings: Finding And Following An Authentic Life*. New York: Harmony Books.

Cameron, Julia. 1992. *The Artist's Way: A Spiritual Path To Higher Creativity*. Los Angeles, CA: Jeremy P. Tarcher/Perigee.

Whitworth, Laura, Henry Kimsey-House, and Phil Sandahl. 1998. *Co-Active Coaching: New Skills For Coaching People Toward Success In Work And Life*. Palo Alto, Calif: Davies-Black.

Dooley, Mike. 2009. *Choose Them Wisely: Thoughts Become Things*. New York: Atria Books.

TUT's Adventurers Club. "Where philosophy meets adventure and connections are made." www.tut.com/theclub.

Byrne, Rhonda. 2006. *The Secret*. New York: Atria Books; Hillsboro, OR.: Beyond Words Pub.

Losier, Michael J. 2007. *Law Of Attraction: The Science Of Attracting More Of What You Want And Less Of What You Don't*. New York: Wellness Central.

Dyer, Wayne W. 2007. *Change Your Thoughts – Change Your Life: Living The Wisdom Of The Tao*. Carlsbad, Calif: Hay House, Inc.

Godin, Seth. 2007. *The Dip: A Little Book That Teaches You When To Quit (And When To Stick)*. New York : Portfolio.

Godin, Seth. 2008. *Tribes: We Need You To Lead Us*. New York: Portfolio.

Godin, Seth. 2003. *Purple Cow: Transform Your Business By Being Remarkable*. New York: Portfolio.

Godin, Seth. 2003. *Linchpin: Are You Indispensable?* New York: Portfolio.

Godin, Seth. 2007. *Meatball Sundae : Is Your Marketing Out Of Sync?* New York: Portfolio.

Jobs, S. (2005, June). Commencement address by Steve Jobs. Retrieved February 14, 2010, from the Stanford University Web site: www.news-service.stanford.edu/news/2005/june15/jobs-061505.html

Jobs, S. (2005, June). Commencement address by Steve Jobs [Video File]. Video posted to: www.youtube.com/watch?v=D1R-jKKp3NA

Michalowicz, Mike. 2009. *The Toilet Paper Entrepreneur*. New Jersey: Obsidian Press

Breinigsville, PA USA
03 August 2010

242935BV00003B/1/P

9 780984 455904